BILLY BARNSTORM,
THE BIRCH LAKE BOMBER

BILLY BARNSTORM,
THE BIRCH LAKE BOMBER

By Joel M. Vance

Books by Joel M. Vance

Grandma and the Buck Deer
Down Home Missouri
Tails I Lose
Autumn Shadows

Available from Cedar Glade Press, Box 1664, Jefferson City, MO 65102. Add $3/book for S/H. Also see www.joelvance.com for e-books not in print and an entertaining blog.

Dedicated to the town of Birchwood, Wisconsin,
(the real Birch Lake) and all the fine folks
who live there.

Author's Note

The town is real; the characters are not.
Anyone who recognizes himself or herself in these
pages is mistaken or has been too deeply into the
Bruenigs Lager. On the other hand, it could have
happened. After all Mr. Eisenhower was the
President and did fish the Brule River....

Five Valleys Press
6240 Saint Thomas Dr.
Missoula, Montana 59803
www.FiveValleysPress.com
info@fivevalleyspress.com

Library of Congress Control Number: 2011932473
International Standard Book Number: 978-0-9835442-2-7

Contents

ANATOMY COMES TO BIRCH LAKE

It is the middle 1950s, long ago. Birch Lake begins to slumber in mid-June and doesn't really wake until the first cold night of autumn. The lake turns to pea soup and fish sull in the dark depths. The mid-day sun is painfully bright and the thick, hot air smells of road tar and lake algae. Labrador retrievers drowse listlessly in the shade, twitching with fevered dreams of icy water and mallards tumbling from the sky.

Summer is the time of the tourist, those strange beings from other worlds—like Indiana and Illinois. My Uncle Floyd's bar fills with visitors in Hawaiian shirts and baseball caps who brag about big fish they've caught. Uncle Floyd, the owner and bartender, arbitrates arguments over the Chicago baseball teams and the Green Bay Packers and Chicago Bears. He is regarded warily by the ladies of the United Church.

True, he owns a bar, a cause for concern, but he also is a member of the town's most revered family. My grandmother is a Birch Lake pioneer and a figure of unassailable rectitude. One does not lightly attack her family.

The Pioneer Days' planners made Uncle Floyd chairman of the midway entertainment subcommittee…and he brought Flame LaTouche to town.

The owner of the previous year's carnival was in jail for kiting bad checks, so Birch Lake needed a new show, preferably one with class. Uncle Floyd was up against it because if there was one thing the Bluegill Bar lacked it was class. He should have known better than to trust a stranger from The Cities who ordered yet another Bruenig's Lager and said, "Trust me, you can't go wrong with the Miller Brothers outfit. I used to work for them guys and they is first rate!"

The deadline loomed and Uncle Floyd was desperate. Uncle Floyd went for the bait. He arranged for the carnival visit over the phone and in time a shabby collection of flatbed trucks and trailers pulled onto Main Street and began to set up some indifferent rides like a Tilt-a-Whirl that looked more bent than tilted, and a miniscule Ferris Wheel that creaked arthritically and wobbled like a wheel with loose lug nuts.

One tired old lion slumbered in a small cage, looking as if it wanted only to sleep or perhaps to die. A group of monkeys threw shit at the onlookers which effectively limited their appeal.

For us randy teenagers Flame LaTouche was the exception to the general decrepitude of the event. She was advertised as "An Exotic Dancer Direct From The Nile!" and she was the flame (or Flame) to our randy crowd, awash in juvenile hormones.

My cousin Hal and I stared at the posters tantalizingly offering glimpses of her charms with the rapt attention our biology teacher had vainly tried to get us to show in class.

"Exotic dancing," Hal declared as if he knew all about it, "means she does sex stuff."

"That's erotic dancing," I said, having made a study of such things since my voice began to change. "Exotic dancing means she does stuff from Bali or Afghanistan or some place like that in the South Pacific."

The United Church League ladies demanded that the performance be prohibited, but the city officials and county court, exclusively men who secretly planned to sneak a peek at Flame

LaTouche, weren't about to ban her exotic Afganistanian gyra-
tions.

They cited the First Amendment, as well as artistic expression. "You ladies don't have to go, you know," said the presiding
commissioner, praying they wouldn't.

The ladies gritted their teeth, mostly false, and stalked
from the meeting to confront my grandmother. "It's your son
who's bringing that...that woman here!" exclaimed Mrs. Ethel
Warburton, a widow, though it always amazed me that some
man could have found her attractive enough to marry. "I
should think you'd be more Christian than to allow it."

My grandmother bristled at the suggestion she was un-
Christian and also that one of her sons might be flawed, although they all were in charming ways. "Floyd is 46 years old,"
she declared, just short of a snarl. "I quit spanking him quite a
few years ago."

Mrs. Warburton huffed off with her doughty delegation and
prayed for salvation. She thought it had come when a rusty
Ford van limped into town. The Rev. Roy Lee Snyder was a
free-swinging revivalist whose biannual visit to Birch Lake just
happened to coincide with that of the Miller Brothers sideshow.

Faced with an implacable phalanx of righteous church ladies, the county court let Brother Snyder set up his revival tent
at the edge of the Midway, figuring that while the town wives
were being saved the husbands could roam the Midway, awkwardly shooting basketballs at a goal half regulation size, firing
a .22 at tin targets that refused to topple...and skulking into
the dark corners of Flame LaTouche's crimson tent, a tent lit by
flickering lamps that made their eyeballs glitter.

Hal and I were throwing rocks at a poster advertising the
visit of Brother Snyder when his rusty van jerked to a stop
beside us. There was an ill-painted sign skewed to the side of
it reading "Jesus Saves!"

"At the Birch Lake Bank," Hal snickered.

"Geez!" I said, "that's blasphemy stuff. Don't make jokes
like that."

"You boys! Get over here!" Brother Snyder had the eye of a raptor, sharp and hungry. He crooked a long finger at us that reminded me of an illustration I'd seen in a Weird Tales Magazine of the Grim Reaper beckoning a lost soul. My mouth went dry.

"Whayuh is the fairgrounds?" the lean preacher asked, a hint of the South and dusty gravel roads in his raw voice. He needed a haircut and a shampoo wouldn't have hurt either. He was at least a day short of a shave and I thought of a buzzard perched in a tree over a road kill.

Hal, who never met a stranger he couldn't irritate, pointed down the road. "Can't miss it," he said. "It's where the hootchy-kootchy dancer is." He did a clumsy shimmy and Brother Snyder's eyes narrowed dangerously.

"Do you attend church, boy?" he growled. We stirred uneasily because while we did go to church it was not a matter of choice. I suspected it didn't qualify as real churchgoing.

"I see sin in you boys," Brother Snyder said. "Oh, I fear you are whoring and gambling and lost!" he exclaimed, wrong on all counts. But he was just warming up. He drew a tattered Bible from his coat jacket as quick as John Wayne ever unholstered a Colt Peacemaker.

Brother Snyder grabbed my arm. It felt like a huge eagle had me in its talons. "Lust is in your heart, boy!" he hissed and reflexively I shut my eyes so he couldn't see in. He had me pegged. I could smell his breath. It was as if he had been snacking on Hell. "Repent or suffer as the damned!"

I was suffering already but just as I was on the verge of blubbering repentance, he let go of me. "Thou shalt regret thy sins and become whole!"

He clambered back into his van and was gone in a flurry of dust.

"Shazaam!" Hal exclaimed. "What a weirdo." I rubbed my arm.

We resumed our study of the poster immediately adjacent to Brother Snyder's, the one advertising the forbidden charms of

Flame LaTouche. Meanwhile Brother Snyder set up his revival tent as close to the Midway as he could get, not realizing it was only a few steps from that of the evil Ms. LaTouche. Dangerous business, like storing explosives close to an open Flame.

The Pioneer Days' fair began and the bay of the calliope and the racket of the sideshow barkers mingled strangely with the preacher exhorting his sweating faithful through a sound system that occasionally screamed like a gutshot tomcat.

The United Church ladies swayed as one, inspired by Brother Snyder's fervent rhythm. A couple of husbands, incompetently evasive, glowered uncomfortably, wishing they were sucking up Bruenig's Lager and drooling over the charms of Flame LaTouche next door.

Charlie Pete, the town drunk, wandered into the revival tent on the second night of the Fair and the holy man threw him out. Charlie Pete was a Chippewa Indian, coppery and seamed, with an unkempt pony tail. He would not swat a pesky deer fly. "Get out, you heathen Indian!" shouted the good Brother. "Get thee to Hell with your Godless aboriginal ancestors!"

Charlie Pete, half in the bag, didn't understand much of what the foam-mouthed preacher was shouting, but he did understand he wasn't wanted. The preacher stalked the spooked Indian like a panther after a deer and Charlie bolted through the tent door, caromed off the rusty van and fell to the ground. Hal and I hauled him to his feet. "What the hell was that all about?" Charlie said, rubbing his forehead. "What'd I ever do to him?" He dabbed at a cut on his forehead with a dirty handkerchief.

"Whyn'cha put some Jibway curse on him?" Hal asked. "Make him turn blue or something."

"Kid, I run outa magic before I was your age," Charlie said. "I need a brew." He wandered off in the direction of town and the Bluegill Bar, familiar territory.

"Poor ol' guy," I said. "That preacher don't have no reason to push him around." We sighed at the incomprehensibility of adults and wandered toward the forbidden tent. I heard the raucous bray of the barker and my hormonal juices escalated to flood spate. "Awright, step inside and see the sweetest thing this side of Vegas!" he shouted. "You kids, move on out, come back when you're old enough to appreciate fine art...and bring money! You get right in to see our little Flame...not only see, I'm telling you...but experience something you'll never experience right here in Birch City."

He got the name of the town wrong, but that was a trifle compared to what our imaginations added to his peroration. He talked over our heads to the adults behind us and, embarrassed by the attention, we slunk to the next tent where a pimpled, greasy guy, scarcely older than we were, implored us to knock down stacked milk bottles and win a purple panda.

I couldn't stand it anymore. "Let's go see her," I said. Hal looked at me, alarmed. For all his bravado he tended to fade into the woodwork when push came to shove. And he knew of my tendency to get into cataclysmic fixes. He believed I could break Jell-o.

"You chicken?" I challenged. That, of course, is the ultimate flung gauntlet to a teenage boy.

"Up yours!" he replied eloquently. We circled behind the Flame LaTouche tent. It was dark back there, untouched by the Midway lights. The tent was quiet, between shows. We cautiously peeked through a gap between two panels in the tent.

"Would you look at that!" Hal hissed. The tent was deserted...and Flame LaTouche's tasseled brassiere was draped over a folding chair. "Talk about a trophy!" Hal breathed. "Go get it."

"Me! You go get it!"

"Shhhh! Shut up and listen. I'll go stand at the front of the tent and if anyone starts to come in, I'll give the Bobcat Bark and you run like hell."

"How come you get to stay outside and I get to go in?" I asked.

"Cause you can't do a good Bobcat Bark," Hal said. "Your voice don't work right. Now quit foolin' around and get in there before somebody comes back."

He vanished around a corner of the tent and I peered in at the spangled brassiere. My mind dwelled on the contents for which those glittering cups were designed and I took a deep and shuddery breath.

Well, what the hell, I thought. I wriggled through the narrow gap in the tent wall and paused inside, my nerves singing like chorus frogs.

I reached for the brassiere and a voice rasped just behind me. "What the hell are you doing!" I completed my grab and whirled to behold Flame LaTouche. She was in the all-together and there was no doubt she was all together. Flame LaTouche was not a modest woman. She covered none of her charms. I breathed, "Shazaam!" and my mouth stayed open. I clutched the brassiere against my chest as if I were the one who was naked, not her.

Flame LaTouche was one angry exotic dancer. "Gimme my bra, you little pissant!" she snarled. She started toward me, raising her hand to display long crimson fingernails, like bloody claws.

I yelped in alarm and dove for the opening in the tent, but missed it. I rebounded off the stiff canvas like a trampoline artist into Ms. LaTouche who exclaimed "oooofff!" and grabbed me as we both lost our balance.

We staggered across the tent and, even in my terror, I realized that naked women were soft in delightful ways not experienced when dancing with clothed ones. We fell over a low table and broke apart and I scrambled to my feet, facing Ms. LaTouche, who seized a book from the table and threw it at me.

I'd been catching for the Birch Lake Cookies for years and I shagged the sailing book one-handed and now grasped two items belonging to Flame LaTouche (not, however, the two I'd been fantasizing about).

Flame LaTouche spoke to me in a way that only the Birch

Lake Bobcat coach had done previously. I figured it was long past time to hit the road and dove again for the gap in the tent and squirted through it with Flame LaTouche hot behind me, a turn of phrase that in more reflective times, would have torched my hormones.

After the glare of the tent lights I was blinded in the dark and squinted desperately, trying to locate a refuge. "Little bastard!" Flame LaTouche roared behind me. I leaped forward, rebounded off a tent support wire and once again found myself in a desperate embrace with a naked woman. Her claws whispered past my ear and I realized she wanted more than her possessions back—she wanted to hurt me.

I wriggled free and saw a sliver of light from under the edge of a nearby tent. I had led the Cookies in base-stealing and sprinted toward the light as if trying to steal second base on Yogi Berra. I dove under the gaping tent bottom and lay for an instant, breathing hard.

And then, piling terror upon terror, someone roughly hauled me to my feet. It was Brother Snyder and again I smelled his breath only this time it strangely carried the aroma of the Bluegill Bar. "What are you doing in my tent!" he growled, gripping my arm painfully in the same place as before. Bruises on bruises.

Caught somewhere between Heaven and Hell, as it were, my mind went out of gear like a worn out transmission on a steep uphill grade. I was wild-eyed with fright. Brother Snyder glared at me. I didn't know what to do, so I thrust the brassiere and book at him like an offering. I noticed that the book was Mickey Spillane's Kiss Me Deadly. Apparently Flame LaTouche and I shared the same literary hero.

Automatically Brother Snyder took the two items and as he realized what he was holding let go of my arm. I sprinted for the door just as it was thrust aside by none other than Mrs. Ethel Warburton, pillar of the United Church ladies and stout guardian of Birch Lake morality.

With the quick move that had made me a minor legend as

a guard for the Bobcats, I juked to one side and pivoted against the tent wall, breathing hard.

Flame LaTouche had slithered through the gap in the back wall with an agility born from years of exotic dancing, and she and The Rev. Snyder were frozen face to face, as if in a waxworks. Mrs. Warburton's coterie of church ladies crowded in behind her, astonished by the inimitable exhibition before them.

Perhaps they thought someone had been saved.

Someone had. Me. "Shazaam!" I breathed again.

"Gimme my goddam bra, you scuzzbutt!" snarled the naked Flame LaTouche. The Rev. Snyder handed it to her, much as I had passed it along to him. He retained the Spillane book, whose provocative cover was clearly visible in the harsh light. The church ladies exclaimed wordlessly in unison.

I waited no longer. I slid sideways along the tent wall and scooted through the door. The aimless clatter of the Midway was a relief after the intense scene inside. Hal appeared out of the dark and hissed, "Did you get it?"

"No," I said. "But that ol' preacher's gonna."

The Rev. Snyder, of course, was discredited and dismissed. He packed his rusty van and vanished from our lives. Flame LaTouche's reputation was enhanced. Her tent was packed every night with those who had heard the story, or so we heard—we didn't go back.

The Fair faded in memory, but there were times that summer when, in the moments just before sleep, I would remember embracing that naked woman. My imagination neatly trimmed her talons and turned her expression from steaming rage to melting affection.

Toward autumn just before school started Hal and I were chunking rocks at the same street sign where we'd first seen the preacher and I looked at the now-tattered poster of Flame LaTouche and took a deep shuddery breath.

"Do you suppose Charlie Pete really can put curses on people?" I asked Hal.

BILLY BARNSTORM, THE BIRCH LAKE BOMBER

I think there must be a gene somewhere in the genetic makeup of all boys, a Girl Trouble code. It surfaces periodically and, like measles, mumps or other childhood mishaps, causes problems. Perhaps the gene is recessive and skips a generation or two or maybe it is dormant. Some boys attract girls without trying and streak through life as if flying on new racing skates, as graceful as birds, as successful as an Olympic gold medalist.

Then there are the kids like me who invariably skate onto the thin ice and ignore the creaking and cracking until it's too late.

My girl troubles began when Billy Barnstorm came to town, the Birch Lake version of the Lone Eagle himself, Charles Lindbergh. The era of the barnstorming aviator was nearly gone by the 1950s; only a few hardy daredevils continued to thrill (or bore) rustic crowds with their aerobatics.

I was thundering into puberty, awash in juvenile hormones and as gauche as a yearling boar hog. It was before Flame LaTouche opened my eyes to the wonders of female flesh and before my libido created phantasmagoric fantasies that had no more chance of realization than my pre-pubescent dream to pitch for the Chicago White Sox who, God knows, could have used a good pitcher.

It was the butt-end of my Age of Innocence and the dreary dawn of a string of haphazard romances as erratic as the course of a pinball down one of the machines in the Bluegill Bar.

It began, as so many doomed romances do, in the spring and I was lovesick. My second cousin, Maeve, was the target of my love bombs, all of which were duds. I had been puppy-sick with love for her since I was old enough to tell that girls were more than boys with longer hair who couldn't throw a baseball worth a damn, even before because she had been my babysitter.

She held my tiny hands when I took tentative, wobbly steps, and gradually let go and I was on my own as I tottered toward the far end of our front room, where my mother waited, her eyes shining. It wasn't that I hadn't had girl friends before—but they were "friends," like boys. Debbie Miller was all tomboy and could throw hard enough to sting your hand.

Maeve was…different. She was a definite she, without scabs on her knees and with little interest in playing burnout. She was Nordic blonde with an impish catlike face and eyes that promised the kind of fun you couldn't read about in 1950. When she hugged me, which was often because she was a hugger, my face burned.

Maeve was tough on boys. By the time she was 16 she had gone through three boyfriends and three automobile accidents, one with each. She'd been driving all three times, although she wasn't old enough the first two times and had a suspended license the third time. The accidents tore apart both the automobiles and the affairs. The boys drifted away to more conventional relationships—duller maybe, but a whole lot safer.

"I don't mean to be wild," Maeve told my aunt. "I just get to having fun." She hugged her mother, my older cousin. No one could stay angry at Maeve. She was as carefree and beautiful as a butterfly. I stood by the door, aching with feelings I couldn't identify—but I knew it wasn't a summer cold.

"Come on, hotshot!" she called, spying me. "Let's go boat riding!" We took my uncle's Chris Craft, the fastest boat on

Birch Lake, and spent the afternoon racing up and down the five-mile-long lake at top speed. She took the Narrows into Balsam Lake, a twisting channel clogged with cabins, docks and water weeds, fast enough to give a dirt track racer palpitations.

Near dusk she cut the throttle somewhere north of Penny Island and the boat wallowed in the wash. We drifted in the lee of the island. We watched the sun setting behind the distant veneer mill. "You ever want to ditch Birch Lake and see what's out in the big ol' world?" she said.

"I don't know. I guess," I said. "I don't know enough about it to decide."

"Well, it's bound to be better than waiting all year for the Pioneer Days' parade and getting hammered on Bruenig's," she said. "If that's the best Birch Lake has I want somewhere else." She was sunburned from the long afternoon, her hair tangled. Her legs were tanned and long and her T-shirt advertising the Bluegill Bar was too small....or just right, depending on how you looked at it. And I had trouble not looking at it.

Betrayed by hormones I sat in the front of the boat as it bobbed in the chop on Birch Lake and tried not to think about that T-shirt. "I don't want you to go off somewhere," I said, my voice tight.

She looked at me, really looked at me, as she might at a boy whose car she hadn't yet wrecked. Maybe Maeve realized for the first time that I wasn't a snot-nosed little kid anymore. She looked flustered, but then gave me the sweet, sad smile of someone who knows an ancient truth. "Aw," she said. "I changed your diapers." I bit my lip and she hauled the anchor.

And then Wild Bill Barnstorm blew into town and changed our lives. No one saw past the flaking paint on his bright yellow airplane to the sad anachronistic man inside. He'd seen the world mostly as a checkerboard of fields and woods and lakes.

Even as I thrilled to his aerobatics, I wanted him to crash and burn because he quickly threatened to take Maeve away from me. He was, we found later, born William Lewis in 1920 in a little Saskatchewan prairie town, so he was pushing 30 when he sailed into Birch Lake, still trying to capture the romance of 1920s aviation when pilots flew by the seat of their britches and every flight was a perilous adventure.

He mourned that he'd been born too late to join the Lafayette Escadrille during World War One and he'd been barely old enough to fly in World War Two, even though he got halfway through flight training before he had managed to crack up a Stearman trainer and jimmy up his back enough that he was medically prohibited from flying then or in Korea. Age and infirmity had kept him out of three wars and all he could do was to challenge fate in risky old airplanes with no one shooting at him.

Billy Lewis could fly an airplane, but there was no one left to fight and he looked toward a grim and dreary future on the grim and dreary Canadian prairie and shuddered. So he bought a second hand plane for a few dollars and became a barnstormer, flying the rickety crate from town to town, entertaining the hayseeds. He changed his name to Wild Bill Barnstorm. He'd buzz the town until the locals gathered on the main street, looking up with their mouths agape and then he'd land in some farmer's pasture and charge $15 for a 15 minute ride.

The passengers would gawp over the rim of the cockpit (a few also would vomit disgustingly, creating interesting abstract art on his brilliant yellow fuselage). Their eyes would water as they saw their little town as no one ever had before.

Billy upgraded his aircraft over the years. During the 1940s he had a stubby racer which he flew in the few aerobatic shows still operating, slaloming around the pylons in daring sharp turns, dangerously close to the ground.

And then Wild Bill came to Birch Lake, another dinky town on his bumpy flight to nowhere. Real pilots were flying jets in Korea and here he was flying a canary yellow Ryan Sport Trainer from the 1930s with open cockpits, one for the pilot, one for a passenger. Wild Bill was an armored knight in a world of Patton tanks. Modern warfare had outgrown the days when Thor's disciples flew fabric covered biplanes all of 80 miles an hour and shot at each other with handguns.

Wild Bill was nearly 30 and my cousin Maeve was 25. I didn't understand why she would hang around with an old man, although commonsense told me that five years difference was no difference at all.

Although Maeve was 11 years older than me, I didn't see that age difference in the same light as I saw the gap between her and Billy Barnstorm. Maeve seemed more a kid than a grownup, while Wild Bill was a time traveler, arrived from decades past and slightly bewildered by the world he dropped into. If Maeve thought of me as a little kid, why couldn't she think of Wild Bill as an old man?

On his introductory flight, Wild Bill circled Main Street with the agility of a hunting mink, his engine roaring, scarcely higher than the steeple on the Methodist Church. By the time he buzzed the town three times everyone had spilled out of the Bluegill Bar, the Get 'Em Bait Shop across the street, the First Savings Bank, Bamburger's Grocery and Drugs and the hardware store to see just what in the hell was going on.

Wild Bill cut the engine, did a roll and let the plane drop like a rock as the crowd gasped. He restarted the engine at the last possible instant and made a feathery landing in Alf Norgaard's alfalfa pasture a quarter mile outside town. The crowd ran to the field, jostling and gawking at this living museum exhibit. The logo on the fuselage read "Wild Bill Barnstorm."

Wild Bill himself climbed from the cockpit, perched his goggles on his leather helmet and surveyed the crowd. He was as lean as Gary Cooper with a seamed, tanned face and eyes as blue as a cloudless summer day. He wore a yellow silk scarf that looped around his neck and trailed down his back. He was as romantic a figure as Wyatt Earp and just as dated.

The back of his leather jacket was decorated with a painting of World War One biplanes dogfighting. The paint was cracked and the jacket needed a liberal application of saddle soap. He pulled a tattered sign from the cockpit that read "Rides $15, 15 minutes."

Even as he planted the sign Maeve was standing in front of him, blonde hair shining like the sun, hands on her hips. "I'll go!" she said. They looked at each other as if neither ever had seen anything quite so astounding.

"Good Godalmighty, she's gonna wreck airplanes now!" grumbled my Uncle Al, remembering her one woman contribution to the local salvage yard. He looked at me. "Between you and her you could screw up a one-car funeral," he said. "What the hell's the matter with this family anyway?"

Maeve ran to me and said, "You got any money? I'll pay you back!" I had $20 lawnmowing money and I fished the crumpled bill out of my jeans and handed it to her. She grabbed my hand and dragged me over to Wild Bill. "Can my cousin and me both get in?" she asked. "He's worth about five bucks and here's my fifteen. I can sit on his lap." I would have paid the whole $20 for that.

Wild Bill was dubious, but Maeve talked him into it. We crawled into the tight cockpit and I scrooched down and Maeve wriggled onto my lap. She donned a pair of intercom earphones and soon was talking to Wild Bill in the front cockpit. I couldn't hear either side of the conversation, but Maeve giggled, and Billy Barnstorm revved the engine and taxied to the far end of the field. I didn't know where to put my hands—on her hips, around her waist.

Maybe it was the alfalfa in the field or maybe it was her but I smelled the essence of summer in Birch Lake, a perfume that spelled enchantment and sunshine. The crowd jostled to the side of the field to give us room for takeoff. Then we swung 180 degrees and Wild Bill stood on the brakes and juiced the engine to a mind-rattling shriek.

He released the brakes and we jounced down the field. I couldn't see anything past Maeve, but her hair streamed in the slipstream into my face and I could see enough over the low side of the cockpit to glimpse the crowd. Then they were below us and the bouncing stopped and we were airborne.

The engine quieted to a comfortable snarl and I peeked over the edge of the cockpit to see my world dropping away as if it would vanish. I gulped and forgot about the lovely girl in my lap. I was transfixed by the miracle of flight. We circled the town and the lake. Billy banked and I saw my grandmother's house and our house, far below. And the Bluegill Bar! A Soo Line freight was crossing the spidery railroad bridge at the Narrows. A fisherman near Snake Island waved as Wild Bill buzzed him. The angler reached over the side of his boat and hoisted a sizeable pike. It looked like a minnow from our vantage point.

I was exhilarated beyond anything I'd ever known. Maeve murmured into the intercom. Just beyond Maeve's shoulders I could see Wild Bill's back and a bit of the painted dogfight on his jacket. And I could see the reason for a jacket because even in the heat of summer the open cockpit was chilly with the wind of our passing. Maeve's soft warmth, though, was better than any old jacket, even one with a battle scene on it.

Wild Bill's yellow scarf streamed back, tickling Maeve's face and when he twisted around enough to give her a huge grin, she grinned back and rubbed the silky softness against her cheek.

The flight was over all too soon. We drifted toward the alfalfa field and then the wheels touched down and we bounced over the rough surface to a stop. Maeve scooted out of my lap and leaped lithely to the ground. I followed and started walking toward the crowd and then became aware that Maeve wasn't with me. I turned and saw her close to Wild Bill and she held his hands in hers.

They were talking. And then they climbed back into the yellow plane, Maeve by herself in the back cockpit, Wild Bill in front. As the astonished crowd looked on (no less astonished than I was), Wild Bill taxied again to the end of the field, whirled and took off again. We all watched as the little plane

climbed steeply toward the distant Blue Hills, became a bright
yellow spark against the clear blue sky and then was gone.
Only a very faint engine whisper lingered and then it too was
gone, leaving an awed hush behind.

"Where the hell did they go?" growled my Uncle Al at me, as
if I could explain my wild cousin. I shrugged, my heart weep-
ing. Something far more romantic than a Birch Lake buck with
a wreckable car had claimed Maeve this time. I swallowed my
heartbreak. Maeve was...Maeve.

So she had changed my diapers a lifetime ago. Now I was
14 years old, a man in all but experience. Wild Bill had managed to fire my imagination and steal my secret love, all in 15
minutes. They returned at dusk. They'd flown to The Cities,
Maeve said breathlessly at dinner that night while I pushed at
my mashed potatoes and felt my heart breaking. They'd circled
Minneapolis and St. Paul, saw the Mississippi and Minnesota
rivers and then raced the setting sun to make it back to Birch
Lake before dark.

"We flew so low we even saw where somebody hit a deer
on the highway, leaving a blood streak like a questionmark!"
Maeve exclaimed, her eyes shining like sunsparks on the riffled
water of Birch Lake. "He said he wanted to fly me to the sun,"
Maeve said. "No one ever said anything that romantic to me
before." Fly to the sun! I couldn't even walk her to the Bluegill
Bar for a beer.

Over the next few days Wild Bill shook what dollars he
could out of Birch Lakers, giving them their 15 minutes of exal-
tation before bringing them back to earth and reality. He also
hit the little towns around, milking them dry. He barely made
gas money, but it kept him close to Maeve. Each evening he'd
fly into Norgaard's pasture and Maeve would meet him and I'd
hear the growl of the engine and see the bright plane heading
toward the clouds.

Maeve's heart seemed to soar with the plane while mine
crashed like the Red Baron, shot full of holes. And then Maeve
dumped Wild Bill. It was abrupt and puzzling. Wild Bill made

his usual evening landing in the pasture but she wasn't there
to meet him. He showed up at our house and talked her into
a walk in the garden. They spent a long time out there among
the tomatoes and raspberry bushes.

Finally he trudged off, his head down, his shoulders
slumped like those of a farmer plowing with horses. I found
Maeve out behind the barn, petting Uncle Al's donkey. She
sniffled and fed the donkey a carrot from the garden. "What
kind of life is flying around scaring cows," she said.

"You thought it was pretty neat the last couple of weeks," I
said ungraciously. She fed the last of the carrot to the donkey
and wiped her hands on her jeans. I took a deep breath and
blurted. "You could stay in Birch Lake and marry me!" The
words hung in the air like a condemned just after the trap is
sprung. "I mean when I get old enough," I added weakly.

She didn't laugh, which was a measure of her wonder.
"You're my cousin," she said. "We'd probably have kids with
two heads."

"Second cousin," I said.

"Whatever." She sniffled again and raised her T-shirt hem
and wiped her nose. I saw the bottom of her bra. She looked at
me. "He looks like daddy," she said.

"Uncle Jack?" I said, confused. Uncle Jack was a shambling
drunk in his 70s, shoulders eternally hunched against a wind
that only he felt. Uncle Jack was a binge drinker, sober most of
the time, but even then looking at his world with scared eyes.

Maeve looked at me and said, "If I didn't love you I wouldn't
tell you this and if you ever repeat it I'll kill you." She turned
toward the house and I followed her inside and up the stairs
to her bedroom. A pair of peach-colored panties were draped
over the only chair in the room and I took a deep breath and
remained standing. It seemed intrusive to sit down on them.
Maeve picked up a framed photo from her dresser and said,
"This was daddy, 35 years ago."

The resemblance was uncanny. The man in the photo was
in the stiff uniform of a World War One soldier, but you could

have dressed Wild Bill in an identical uniform, put them side by side and you'd have had trouble telling them apart. I had no idea that Uncle Jack had been in the Great War, but that was two wars ago and long forgotten...except, I suspected, by Uncle Jack. But in the photo he looked at the camera with insolent confidence, knowing he was braver and tougher than any of those cowardly Huns.

I compared that image with the reality of the perpetu-ally frightened old man I knew and exclaimed, "That's Uncle Jack!" She nodded. "If I had to fall for someone in a uniform, why couldn't it have been the God damn postman," she said. "I didn't even think about it until I looked at this picture. You can't marry your daddy."

Maeve confessed to no one else, especially to Wild Bill. She just told her mother that things didn't work out and her mother tightened her lips and gave Maeve a hug. Uncle Jack just looked scared.

Two days later Wild Bill stopped me on the street near the Bluegill Bar and declared, "I ain't goin' down without a fight! I never crashed before and I ain't gonna start with that little gal. And you're gonna help me. You're family."

"Why should I?" I asked. "You'll just take Maeve off some-where."

"Because I'll fry your balls if you don't," he replied, look-ing every bit ready to do just such a thing. It was a power-ful argument. He explained his plan, such as it was, and I thought that's the dumbest thing I ever heard. He said he had tried to rent a smoke-writing plane in Minneapolis so he could write "Maeve, marry me!" in the sky above Birch Lake, but he couldn't find one.

Instead he had printed 5,000 leaflets, enough for two for every man, woman and child in Birch Lake. He handed me one which read, "I love you, Maeve! Will you fly away with me for-ever!" There was a badly printed illustration filling the rest of the page, but Wild Bill must have been on short time and stuck for inspiration, for it was a scene of a dogfight among a whirl of ancient biplanes—not exactly a picture from epic romance. The rest of the leaflets were in a bundle, tightly fastened with twine.

Wild Bill's plan involved the Pioneer Days' parade which just happened to coincide with his love quest. That parade would, in years to come, feature prominently in the continuing saga of my romantic disasters. It became a time of year when I arranged to be far from town, trout fishing on some trickle where even the Mounties couldn't have found me.

On the day that Wild Bill planned his Quixotic flight it was clear and bright, a Norman Rockwell sky (as it turned out painted by Charles Addams). "You get in the back and put the headphones on," he ordered. "When I give you the signal you drop the leaflets. Got it?" I nodded, as happy as if he were ordering me to jump out instead of the leaflets…without a parachute.

We took off from the bumpy cow pasture and the old plane creaked and groaned like an over-the-hill athlete trying to warm up for one more game. Then we were in the air and I peered over the rim of the cockpit to Birch Lake below. Wild Bill banked sharply and I gulped and swallowed a sudden rush of saliva. If motion sickness is in your head, why does your stomach threaten to turn inside-out?

We circled the town that was my world. We passed over the dam and I saw a thin veil of water dropping to the spillway below. Snake Island was a green dot and far beyond was Penny Island where I had pledged my love to Maeve and been rejected.

I'd thought that if I could perform some heroic feat Maeve would realize that I was her destiny. It was fantasy right out of an Errol Flynn movie at the Rialto. My little world was circumscribed by such Hollywood fantasies since I had no experience farther away than Edgewater to the North or Rice Lake to the South. But instead of Captain Blood on the deck of a privateer, I was Assistant Flunky on a flaking airplane and instead of winning the girl of my dreams I was the unwilling accomplice of someone who was out to steal the girl of my dreams. Thus does reality bump aside fiction?

How could I compete anyway? Here was Wild Bill, a romantic figure out of breathless fiction and here was I, a callow kid with hayseeds stuck in his hair. I couldn't fly an airplane, couldn't even legally drive a car, was wearing my cousin's hand-me-down blue jeans. I had big ears and the savoir faire of a Duroc shoat.

Wild Bill's voice crackled in my ears, tinny and distant. "Look down," he said. I did and saw Main Street several hundred feet below, a jumble of color and motion. I could make out the pale ovals of faces looking up at us. Wild Bill buzzed the crowd and then we climbed and banked. "Get ready!" he said into the intercom. He gave me a thumbs up signal over his shoulder. This would be our bombing run. I lifted the bundle of leaflets onto the rim of the cockpit and felt for my pocket-knife in the tight jeans. It squirted out of my fingertips and I dug deeper in my pocket.

The plane hit an air pocket and dropped and I felt my grip on the bundle slip and it came free of my hand. I grabbed frantically for it...but it was gone! "Whoops!" I exclaimed and Wild Bill craned his neck and looked back at me. He realized what had happened and jammed the plane in a tight turn as if he could intercept the falling bundle but it already was a tiny dot, falling toward Birch Lake's crowded Main Street like the hammer of God.

It plunged through the paper mache bluegill that was the feature of the town's own float, collapsing the fish into a tangle of braces and paper, along with the sign, "Birch Lake, Bluegill Capital of Wisconsin." It bounced into the air and landed in the front seat of the idling convertible holding Debbie Miller, my erstwhile girl friend, who was that year's Junior Miss Bluegill Queen.

The edge of the bundle caught the shift lever, popping the vehicle into "drive," and the powder blue Cadillac lurched forward. Debbie, perched on the rear seat rest in a lovely taffeta formal, was dumped backward onto the trunk, her feet in the air.

She slid down the sloping truck and landed on her butt in the middle of Main Street, sitting there stupefied. Meanwhile the malicious bundle of love leaflets rolled off the front seat onto the accelerator of the driverless automobile. The big Cadillac engine roared and the car leaped forward, tires squalling on the pavement. People screamed and scrambled out of the way. The car caromed off a telephone pole and headed for the Birch Lake Volunteer Fire Squad which was blissfully unaware of the danger bearing down on it since its members were busy competing with Edgewater in the annual Beer Keg hose-of-war event (each team used a fire hose to try to push the suspended beer keg which they had eagerly emptied before the contest over a goal line).

Just as the car was upon them they sensed something wrong and glanced back. All jumped out of the way just in time and dropped the hose. The hose, under full pressure, writhed from one side of the street to the other, knocking spectators down like ten pins. The powerful jet swept across the bandstand, jumbling the equipment of Art Lundgren and the Jackpine Mellotones.

The firemen finally managed to corral their runaway hose. Debbie Miller pulled herself off the pavement with some effort because the hot day had melted the road tar and glued her down. Everyone had seen the bundle of leaflets fall from the plane and everyone knew to whom the plane belonged, including the sheriff, who surveyed the shambles of his once-tranquil town and, with a face as grim as the hangman's, climbed into his cruiser. "I know that crazy bastard can't fly forever," he snarled.

As graphic evidence that when it rains it pours, Wild Bill's little airplane began to cough and sputter, either a victim of bad gas or bad karma. I was wide-eyed with fear. Wild Bill tugged and pulled and struggled with various instruments, his shoulders working like someone wrestling with a pinball machine. The engine quit with a tubercular wheeze and a soft summer wind sang in the wing braces.

Wild Bill peered over the side of his cockpit and he looked old, like the men who sat on the bench in front of the hardware store and spit on the sidewalk. But you don't barnstorm for a couple of decades without learning something about dealing with emergency. Wild Bill coaxed the airplane into the wind and spotted the cow pasture he'd been using as a landing strip.

He brought the plane in as softly as a puppy's cheek. The still-hot engine ticked quietly and we sat in our respective cockpits coming to grips with the fact that we still were alive. I released my seat belt with a noisy click and Bill swung around to face me. "Get the hell out of here, kid! Right now!"

It didn't take much urging. I'd learned early on that the best weapon against looming trouble was to run like hell. I was into the trees at the edge of the pasture by the time the sheriff's car jounced into the pasture, his gumball machine light throbbing.

The sheriff arrested Wild Bill on a variety of charges, some he made up on the spot, including flying in a reckless manner and crossing the center line of Main Street, as well as failing to stop at the light at the edge of town.

I wasn't sure if Maeve ever knew that I was the unwitting (or more accurately the witless) accomplice of her swain or not, but she was remarkably cool to me for a long time. She totally wrote off Wild Bill who managed to pay off most of the damages with the sale of his airplane.

After he got out of the slammer, he left town on a bus and no one came to say goodbye except me. "Well, we had a hell of a time," he said sadly. He got on the bus and he looked really old now. I never saw him again. As for Maeve, she took up with the son of the town butcher, a fat kid who always smelled faintly of tallow and they presently got married and opened a satellite meat market in Rice Lake, 30 miles and a thousand light years away from Birch Lake.

Uncle Jack swore off the bottle. Once I came into their

house thinking no one was home and saw him holding the photograph of himself in uniform. He didn't see me and didn't know that I saw the tears on his face.

I continued into puberty and Debbie Miller, peeled off the pavement, became for better (or as would prove the case, for worse) my girl friend.

DAMNED OLD CAT

Birch Lake lies amid the boreal zone, glacial lakes and conifers dominating. It's midway down a 20-mile long chain of lakes, 150 miles from the Twin Cities and, in the 1950s, light years away from changing times. Joe McCarthy's rantings in the Senate played big downstate, but in Birch Lake the hot topic was whether the Pioneer Days' parade was impressive enough.

The little town depended on tourism and drinking—the tourists came to fish and finish the day at the Bluegill Bar sopping up Bruenig's Lager. The locals mostly dispensed with the fishing part. Just your average north Wisconsin backwater. You'd hear a distant outboard motor on Birch Lake almost any daylight hour, the faint "chunk, chunk, chunk" of some kind of machinery at the veneer mill, kids shouting shrilly in the middle of a summertime game.

I had been one of those kids not so long ago, playing kick the can in the last light of a summer evening. That was when there wasn't much difference between the boys and the girls— we all were flat in front. We'd play until we got thirsty and then stop by Jake's filling station for an icy Coke fished out of the half ice, half water slosh of his cooler.

Jake was the town grease monkey and political pundit.

Even the kids knew he largely was full of it, but we enjoyed listening to him fulminate over politics, religion and fishing, and petting his battle-scarred tomcat, Willie. "I ain't never seen a Democrat fishing," Jake observed, sure in his mind that all his listeners were Republicans. He also had pretty strong feelings about tourists from Illinois and Indiana.

My father was an unreconstructed Democrat and I guessed I probably was, since I'd never known a president who wasn't one (actually, I never knew any who were, but I knew who they were).

The weekend started on Friday which, I guess technically, is not the weekend, but when it's summer vacation just about any day can be a weekend. I was hanging out at Jake's when he went ballistic in the truest sense of the word. That scary episode started the longest weekend and pretty well ended Jake.

I liked Jake, a scruffy old half-assed shade tree mechanic, who had pumped gasoline for Birch Lakers just about since there were automobiles to pump gas for. It was his life and the station was the unofficial hot stove gathering spot for a few old farts and a few kids like me. Good place to hear lies, tall tales and the occasional fact, generally so dosed with fiction that you couldn't recognize it.

"The reason walleye fishin' is off is 'cause the water's too damn hot. And you know why it's hot? 'Cause of them goddam atom bomb tests! Pretty soon the damn well water'll be about like bath water."

Thus spoke Jake to which any of his grubby friends invariably replied, "Bullshit! Horse hockey! Jake, you're full of it."

I liked Jake because he didn't treat me like a dumb kid. Even Scuz Olson liked Jake. He was a good old boy and he had a smart streak that he kept hidden from the dumb customers, but trotted out when it was appropriate. And he liked what he did, pump gas and gas with the customers. He did both really well.

But the Quik Fill intruded on his world like a genuine

UFO, something that we saw reports about nearly every day in the newspapers. This was a real alien, something Birch Lake never had seen and something that threatened the very essence of the little town.

The Quik Fill was a chain filling station and convenience store, one of the first of that insidious breed that crept across the country, gobbling businesses that had existed forever. It was as if Birch Lake were out of equilibrium, tilting to the south end where the Quik Fill was—every stable element of the town was oozing downhill into a pile at the new business.

And it was right across the street from Jake.

Jake's cat, Willie, was a fixture in the grimy filling station office. Willie was a pain-in-the-ass tomcat, like most tomcats. He was big and yellow and scruffy, with torn ears from nocturnal battles. His nose was ever-scabbed. Willie Cat had been whacked around by life's storms. The cat accepted the indignity indifferently, the way it accepted everything.

Willie sat in the window, looking through the scuffed pane at the world outside with resignation or acceptance or who-knows-what. Who can figure a cat? Customers, coming to pay for their gas, pointed and laughed at the cat which looked at them with sleepy indifference.

Jake admired the independence of the cat, even as he realized that Willie owed him nothing. The cat survived life's backhands, scarred, bloody and ruffled, but not beaten. Defeat was not part of a cat. It fought and either lived or died. It was the way of a cat.

Until recently, the cat's view had mostly consisted of an empty lot. Then the Quik Fill Corporation built their glistening tribute directly across from him. We weren't used to corporate America in Birch Lake—in fact this was the first chain store of any kind within 50 miles.

If the feline equivalent of a Quik Fill had moved in on Willie, he'd either have fought it or moved to new territory. Jake, on the other hand, didn't have any idea where or how to start a fight with a corporation and couldn't move.

I fished a bottle of Coke out of the cooler at the rear of the office, the ice water numbing my hand. I popped the cap on the cooler's opener and sat on a cracked-covered stool and watched as Jake moodily went through his morning ritual. He propped open the green-painted door with its small glass panels, gray and yellow flecks in the chipped places from former paint jobs.

On the first really cold morning of autumn he'd light a fire in the potbellied stove, if the God damn birds hadn't nested in the chimney again, but not this morning when it threatened to be in the 90s later on.

Jake looked across the street at the big sign with the gas prices posted. "Shit," he said. "I can't charge those prices without going in the hole. I can't fight city hall. Those suckers got more money than Carter has Little Liver Pills."

I understood in a teenage way that it was hard enough to make a living when Jake was the only filling station on the west end of town and impossible when the Quik Fill moved in and shot the legs right out from under him. I sipped on my Coke while Jake filled a car, washed the windshield and checked the oil.

Everything in the office was grimy with age. There was a John Deere calendar from 1946, frozen at the August page.

Jake and an old farmer came inside and while he made change, Jake growled, "God damn chains anyway. What does the little guy do about it?"

The farmer, with his own problems, said, "Goes to work for 'em, I guess. You oughta try and grow potatoes, you think that's bad. Costs more to raise 'em than you get back." They decided that the Quik Fill was the end of life as they knew it, but Jake suspected it was a matter of time until the farmer pulled into the six pumps at the Quik Fill instead of Jake's Station. A battered pickup thumped through the pothole at the entrance to the station and stopped at the back pump, brakes shrieking slightly. Old man Albright. Jake propped the broom against the gilded cash register and went out, wiping his hands on his overalls.

"Mornin', Ed," he said. Old man Albright grunted. "Fill 'er up?" Jake asked.

"Two bucks worth," the farmer said. "Get me home. Gotta pump there."

"Shit, you plow jockeys with your farm pumps 'bout run me out of business," Jake said, but he said it good-naturedly. Farmers had to watch their cash like him. Couldn't blame them.

"Gettin' hot, ain't it," Jake commented. "How's your corn crop?"

"Needs rain," old man Albright said. "Don't matter much. Don't get enough for it to pay for raisin' it."

"Ain't that the truth, though," Jake said. "Nothin' the way it used to be."

"No, and it ain't ever gonna be again," the old man said. He looked past Jake, bunching his mouth as if he wanted to spit, but Jake was in the way, so he contented himself with a muffled grunt and swallowed.

"Figured you'd be over at that goddamn place across the street, like everybody else," Jake said.

"Don't hold with them places," the old man replied. "I got along without them foreign bastards all my life and I ain't gonna give in now. Might be cheaper, but you don't hardly know what you're gettin'. Damn truck don't hardly run anyway. Don't like them snotty little girls they got workin' there. Can't hardly get waited on, too busy talkin' about boys or gigglin' about some foolishness."

The pump clicked off and Jake made a few ineffectual passes at the bug-splashed windshield. It was a miracle the old man could see to drive. Old man Albright fished in a stiff leather drawstring purse for the gas money, his knobby fingers probing for change.

"You take care, Ed," Jake said.

The old man waved without looking at Jake and pulled the truck into gear. The queasy transmission clanked and the truck lurched forward.

"Had a few hundred more like Ed and I'd make a living in this God damn place," Jake mumbled after the truck. He glanced across the street at the neon sign of the Quik Fill and belched sourly.

His third customer was a stranger, a minor miracle. Strangers didn't stop at Jake's; they went to the Quik Fill. The stranger returned from the rest room, wiping his hands under his armpits, and said, "Hey, Bonnie and Clyde been in here today?"

"What?" Jake said.

"This place," the customer said, nodding at the building. "Right out of the 1930s. You oughta turn it into a museum. I mean it."

Jake replaced the pump nozzle and took a deep breath, as if he were going to say something, but shook his head instead.

"I mean it," The stranger said. "I haven't seen anything like this for probably 40 years. When I was a little kid, my daddy used to stop at a place just like this. "I remember the smell. Grease and dirt and maybe some gasoline mixed in. It's my kid smell, you know the way you never forget things you smelled when you were a kid? Why, I bet people would come in here just to get some nostalgia along with their gas, you was to fix it up." He looked at me. "You know what I mean, kid—gas and grease smell?"

Oddly I did.

But Jake looked at the customer as if he had just sprouted antennae from his forehead and begun roaring like the Frankenstein monster. As if he didn't have enough trouble getting customers, when he did, they're fruity nuts as junkyard rats.

"You ain't serious."

"Sure," the man said. "Hell, nostalgia is in these days. Shit, you got one of those quick stops on every corner, but there's nothing like this."

"You got that right," Jake growled. He snapped his windshield rag.

"So, how long's this place been here?" the man asked.

"My daddy started it in the 1920s," Jake said. "Ran it until almost World War Two. Then I got it and I've been here ever since. Daddy said he never had to mop the floor when I was a baby," Jake said. "I'd keep it shined up by crawling across it with a wet diaper."

"What I'm sayin'," said the stranger. "You got history goin' for you." He laughed and handed Jake his gas money. Jake made change and the customer got in his car. "No kidding, you got a gold mine here."

Jake smiled with no mirth. Gold mine. Oatmeal for brains. He answered the man's departing wave with a half-lifted hand and went back into the station to open a bag of Cheesits that had been on the rack for months. They were stale, but filling and they already were paid for. He pitched me a bag. "On the house."

He looked around the untidy office. "Museum, shit! Spend some money fixin' it up, shit! Bank wouldn't loan me money if I was a Rockefeller unless I gave 'em New York City. Museum, shit!"

He looked across the street at the Quik Fill. All six pumps were occupied. "Coupla them guys used to buy here," he said.

Even as we were looking through the hazy, dirty window, Willie the cat started across the street and a car from Indiana, turning into the Quik Fill, ran over him, squashing him like a toad frog. Jake saw it happen and stiffened and clenched his fists so hard the knuckles tuned white. I didn't know what to say.

"Geez, Jake, that's terrible!" I stammered. "Old Willie..."

"Never liked him much anyway," Jake said. "I'll go get him, bury him out back. He's just a damned old cat." But his voice was more gravelly than usual and it broke at the end.

Jake found a coal scoop in the back of the garage and loaded what was left of Willie on it. He buried him behind the station, near a pile of rusting oil cans that had been there as long as I could remember.

The front window was empty without the cat. Willie had

been part of the station, like the pumps and the wood stove.
"Wasn't that asshole from Indiana ran over Willie," Jake
said. "It was the God damned Quik Fill." He was talking to
himself, not to me. I was forgotten in the corner, extremely
uncomfortable, but half-afraid to get up and leave.

Jake mumbled and stared through the window at the blood
spot in the road that had been Willie. Once he groaned as if
struck by a sudden fierce pain. The emotion was building in
him like steam in a boiler, rapidly escalating into the red zone.

He looked not at me but through me, as if seeing something
far beyond the dirty walls of the station. Then he stalked
stiffly behind the counter and came out with a short double-
barreled shotgun that had been there since his father opened
the place, never used and now rusted and dusty. Jake didn't
bother to check whether it was loaded.

"Jake…" I said in a squeaky voice but he either didn't hear
me or ignored me. He left the door open behind him as he
started across the street to the Quik Fill. I didn't know what to
do and turned in a circle, indecisively on legs suddenly grown
geriatric. My mind was jumbled, a hand grenade of thought
fragments—stop him…call for help…run like hell.

Then I tottered after him, nothing heroic in mind. Just like
a piece of scrap iron eddying after a powerful magnetic field.
Jake marched into the Quik Fill and I stumbled in behind him
and huddled next to the rack of newspapers.

There were two young women behind the counter. One held
her hand over a bleeding pimple. Another wore a bandana to
cover pink curlers. There also were two customers.

"I want to…." Jake said, holding the shotgun at his side,
muzzle down.

"I was here first, buddy," one of the customers said, frowning.

"I want…." Jake began again.

"You'll have to wait your turn, mister," said the girl at the
cash register. She poked at the cash register keys and pouted.
"It ain't workin'," she said to the other girl.

"You gotta hit this," the other girl said, slapping the "No Sale" key. The register clanged open. Jake turned a small, impatient circle.

"So, anyway," the cashier said, fumbling through paper money, "She said that he called and he said there wasn't any reason to call. That he already knew about it and...."

"Hey!" Jake shouted. "I'm gettin' tired uh waitin."

"Well, excuuuuuse me!" exclaimed the cashier with exaggerated courtesy. "We have other customers here, you know. You'll have to wait, sir."

Jake's fury overwhelmed him. He wanted to blast the stupid woman with his shotgun, shoot the Quik Fill logo right off her dirty uniform, turn every one of them to bloody rags. He raised the gun and the woman with the bleeding pimple shrieked, "Oh, my God, he's got a gun!"

Both women began to scream and the two customers dove to the floor. "Shut up!" Jake shouted. "God damn it, shut up!"

But the women continued to squeal, like terrorized shoats and I added a terrified moan. Frustrated, Jake snarled and grabbed a package of Cheesits and a can of Copenhagen smokeless tobacco.

He ran out of the Quik Fill and skipped and hopped in the driveway, overloaded on adrenaline and terror.

He ran to a rusty pickup and tugged at the door, but it was stuck and he kicked it in frustration. The driver of another truck gawked at him from another pump. He ran to the truck and stuck the shotgun against the window. He didn't know what to say.

The driver looked at the twin barrels of the shotgun and at Jake's distorted expression and stepped on the gas. The sideview mirror slapped the shotgun barrel and wheeled Jake around in a tight circle.

There was no one else at the Quik Fill. For once the pumps were empty, save for the sagging pickup with the rusted doors.

Jake ran across the street and into his filling station. He was numb with panic. He sat in the window where the cat once sat, his back to the street and the Quik Fill.

He hummed and rocked with terror. I could imagine what was going through his head: What a stupid, fucking incredible dumb damn thing I've done! What would he give to live the last 20 minutes over again. What would he give? What did he have to give?

I watched as he sat on the window seat, the shotgun in his lap, until the sheriff arrived and banged through the old chip-painted door. "Hold it, Jake!" the lawman shouted. "Just hold it right there!" He jabbed a .45 automatic in Jake's direction.

Jake raised his head and looked at the trembling sheriff who never had confronted an armed man before. Jake shook his head and I heard him through the open door of the filling station. "I never liked that old cat anyway," he said. "He was better off run over."

FALLING FOR YOU

Debbie Miller had been my girl friend all through high school, but the course of true love never is smooth and the argument started over whether I was being unreasonable. Of course I wasn't and she was being unreasonable for saying so. I told her that at the top of my voice after which she spun my head about with a slap that sounded like a .22 long-rifle shot.

Debbie Miller was five-foot-five inches, maybe 105 pounds, but she had a right on her like a contending welterweight and my face hurt for a week. A week during which we did not speak, nor acknowledge the existence of the other. Who needed her? Just because we'd been buddies since we were five years old and just because we'd been dating for three years of high school was no reason for her to ruin my life.

There were plenty of girls just like her...well, on reflection, I hoped maybe not just like her. I could do without the shot to the chops.

I pouted for a few days, considering whether I should apologize but the family's most notable trait—bullheadedness—kept me from it. No doubt about it I missed Debbie. She was petite with a spattering of almost-freckles and startling blue eyes, a blonde ponytail that swished when she walked, an impish smile and whatever shampoo she used, she always smelled like a soft summer evening.

Then I met Becky Ann Garner, she of green eyes and flaming red hair. Becky Ann moved to Birch Lake from a state we considered Deep South—Indiana—when her father was transferred to manage the veneer mill.

It was just before the beginning of my junior year in high school and, as the red marks left by Debbie's hand faded, I realized I had no girl friend. It looked like a long year. Then, in a scene from a Regency romance, as played by Laurel and Hardy, I met Becky Ann.

I had gone fishing, my main remaining activity. Baseball season had ended with us so far out of the playoffs that I didn't even feel like playing catch with Rusty, the Soo Line station agent.

I was three miles from the trailhead on a Forest Service logging trail, heading for a tiny brook trout stream. It was a bright August day, already with a hint of fall in the air. The hike and the cool air sparked my appetite and I began to argue with myself about eating the peanut butter sandwich I had in a day pack. "If you eat it now you'll starve before you get back," I told myself.

"But I'm starving now," I whined to me. "Okay, dummy, I said in reply, "but don't say I didn't tell you." I always managed to win arguments with myself, no matter which side I took. It was a combination of cool logic and weak willpower.

I spotted a mossy old log and plopped down on it, shed my day pack and rummaged in it for the sandwich, wishing I had made more and included a bag of potato chips and a bottle of pop, even though the pop would have gotten warm. I crammed half the sandwich in my mouth and the peanut butter and bread instantly soaked up my saliva and clogged my tongue.

I heard what sounded like distant thunder and paused in my chewing, puzzled. There were no clouds, no hint of a storm. The drumming sound grew steadily louder and I tensed. What the hell was going on?

And then, from around the last bend in the trail came a cantering horse and rider. My mouth would have dropped open had it not been glued shut by the glop of peanut butter.

The horse was okay, as horses go...but the girl atop it was beautiful. Long red hair flowed behind her like a silken scarf. I instantly thought of Lady Godiva and checked, but she was wearing shorts and a blouse. She sat atop the big horse as eas- ily as Duke Wayne himself and a whole lot more attractively. She reined in the horse and looked at me as the horse pranced and yawed at the bit.

She was absolutely lovely—the girl, not the horse. The horse looked wild-eyed and hysterical which is what most horses look like most of the time, or so I thought. The girl was long-legged and tanned and that beautiful, soft red hair draped over her back. Her eyes were emerald green and her lips were strawberries, ripe from the patch.

She opened those lips that were made for the kind of kisses that cause Frenchmen to clutch their bosoms, and spoke: "Hi!"

I tried to swallow, tried to open my mouth to speak, but the peanut butter held me speechbound. My face contorted as my larynx spasmed and I exclaimed a muffled "Moooph!"

The horse sidestepped in alarm. I waved the peanut but- ter sandwich at her and she looked down as if I were waving a machete. In frantic sign language I stabbed at the sandwich with my forefinger, peeled it to show her the peanut butter, pantomimed eating, pointed at my mouth, grabbed my throat to indicate choking...and lost my balance and fell over back- ward on the other side of the log, into a hole just about my size. It was like a bear pit. I couldn't move. My legs waved in the air. I couldn't get purchase with my elbows to pull myself free. The sandwich had flown to God-knows-where.

I heard drumming hoofbeats again and by the time I had floundered free and scrambled to my feet the girl was almost at the bend. I blew out the clot of sandwich and shouted but it was too late. She had vanished around the bend. In frustra- tion I picked up the other half of the sandwich and threw it in the direction they had gone. My stomach growled.

That was it, or so I thought. Not only had I lost my long-time girl friend, I'd lost a red-haired opportunity to find a new one. School was to begin in two days and I brooded over the weekend, feeling like a novice monk with serious reservations.

On Monday morning Becky Ann appeared in the seat next to me in Earth Sciences, my first class. I lacked only a peanut butter sandwich, but did manage to appear dumbstruck and considerably less articulate than Mortimer Snerd, ventriloquist Edgar Bergen's doltish dummy.

She looked cautiously at me. "Aren't you...."

I grimaced. "Peanut butter sandwich. That's what I was trying to tell you. It stuck my mouth all up."

"I thought you were crazy or something. You scared Hero." I looked puzzled. "My horse."

"Your horse is named Hero and he was afraid of a guy with a peanut butter sandwich?" I asked.

She laughed, the sound of a crystal wind chime, and I drew a shaky breath. In the few moments before the teacher began a discussion of turbulent weather I created an emotional storm of my own. "Listen!" I blurted. "Let's go get a Coke or something. No peanut butter sandwiches." She laughed again and angel harps rang.

It was impossible in a high school as small as Birch Lake's not to run into Debbie Miller in the hall and of course I did so immediately after that first class. "Looks like you found a new friend," she said. I shrugged uncomfortably.

We stood silently for about a century and then I cleared my throat. "Listen," I said, "I'm sorry for being such a jerk."

"That's okay," she said. "You've been a jerk before. She paused and bit her lip. "What about Becky Ann? Can she fish?"

"She has horses," I said.

"Well, maybe they'll find a cure for it," Debbie said.

I started to say something and we both spotted Becky Ann in the hall ahead and Debbie said, "Better go tend to your redheaded roan." She left me standing between a rock and a hard place. I took a step after Debbie, then turned and followed Becky Ann.

I quickly found that the key to Becky Ann Garner's heart was "love me, love my horses." She was the first horseperson I had known. Horses hadn't been prevalent in Birch Lake since the logging days, half a century before. There were a few old farm nags living out their days in scant pastures cut into the conifers but those were light years from Becky Ann Garner's spirited gelding. Birch Lakers inclined to outboard motors and pickup trucks for their steeds.

I'd thrilled to John Wayne and Randy Scott riding to the rescue when I was a little kid, but I was less enthusiastic about horses now that I was a teenager, old enough to drive and with my own rusty, beat-up pickup truck. Horses had ceased to be celluloid icons and now they breathed so you could feel it and they did disgusting things where you might walk.

When Becky Ann introduced me to Hero I was toenail to hoof with a large, walleyed creature that immediately stepped on my foot. I yawped with pain and Becky said, "Hero! Now you know better than that."

The horse leaned a little more heavily and tears of pain started in my eyes. Hero looked impassively at me from the corner of his eye. "Get him off me!" I squealed.

"Silly boy!" she said and I didn't know if she meant me or the fucking horse. She tapped Hero on the leg and he obligingly lifted his foot. I staggered back, shards of pain shrieking through my bruised toes.

"He's really a dear," Becky Ann said. "I hope he didn't hurt you."

"It's okay," I gritted, wishing for God to lance that evil bastard with a lightning bolt that would fry him to a crispy horseburger.

Becky moved close to me. The sweet smell of her silken hair and the scent of cologne mingled with a subtle, acrid tinge of horse sweat. I grew faint with infatuation. If it took pretending to like horses to have Becky Ann wrap her aura around me then I'd become Willie Shoemaker.

We became a couple. Head over heels in horse sweat, I was a fool in love. Our first kiss was a lip-smasher that somehow lacked the sweet and familiar softness that Debbie Miller and I shared on our occasional kisses—but I figured passion was supposed to be raw and elemental.

Becky Ann and I dated at least twice a week for a month. I was numb with passion. It was early October and the maple leaves were in full flower. The days were crisp and sunny. On similar days Debbie and I had gone trout fishing on Thirty Three Creek, but not this year—I had a redheaded fish to fry. Sometimes in the halls of Birch Lake High Debbie and I would cross glances, like two knights crossing swords, both cutting and lethal.

Becky Ann invited me to go riding. She had a second horse, a docile mare named Smokey, who had been her kindergarten horse, I guess. Just what I needed: a horse with training wheels.

The mare stood patiently while I fumbled around trying to get on. Mounting a horse is a little bit like climbing a cliff face. They're big and have outcroppings that are hard to get over.

But I finally plunked into the saddle and we were off down a National Forest trail. It was like riding a hay wagon with square wheels. The horse went up when I was coming down and vice-versa. My butt began to feel the way it did long before when my father had whaled the tar out of me for losing his fishing rod.

How could Becky Ann stay with her horse as if she were welded to the saddle? My head began to ache from the incessant pounding and I was relieved when she suggested we stop and picnic. She had brought a picnic lunch in her saddlebags. She spread a blanket on a grassy knoll overlooking Thirty Three Creek and laid out the food. I groaned as I eased my throbbing body onto the blanket.

Debbie and I had picnicked on our trout fishing trips, but

without the horses. She made wonderful sandwiches, juicy and tasty. Much as I loved her, Becky's sandwich had the consistency and taste of corrugated cardboard.

When I finally choked down the last of it, I looked at Becky and she looked at me and it seemed the most natural thing in the world to lean over and kiss her. Her lips were soft and clinging this time, not the hard, challenging kiss of our first time. She fell backward on the blanket, pulling me after her.

I was breathless with lust. It appeared that we were at a moment of crisis in our relationship. This was the tipping point, beyond which there was no return. I was, not to put too fine a point on it, a virgin. If Becky was, it was obvious in body language and soft sighs that she was ready to alter that condition. I was too except for one niggling problem.

I had to piss. Really badly.

You don't have to know much about romance to know that one does not excuse oneself to go whiz when the moment of consummation is at hand. You do not, at the critical moment of passion announce that you have to go to the bathroom. Thinking about it only makes it worse. The urge grew steadily more insistent and my kisses more distracted. "What's wrong?" she murmured, her eyes heavy with passion. "You aren't with me anymore."

"Yes I am!" I cried, kissing her fervently. I squirmed uncomfortably.

`She sighed. "I should be ashamed of myself, but I just can't help it." She looked at me so invitingly my mouth went dry. But my other need was overwhelming. I just couldn't wait another instant.

"I love you!" I groaned, nuzzling at her throat. "But I gotta pee!" I jumped up and ran for the trees, doubled over. Smokey, apparently afraid I was leaving her in the woods with the wolves, trotted along behind me. "Get outta here!" I hissed. "Go on!" The mare snorted and pushed at me with her nose. Apparently she had, like her mistress, fallen in love with me. "Beat it!" I snarled, tugging at my zipper.

I started to take one more step and nearly fell into the creek which was overhung with grass and alders and almost invisible. I recoiled right into Smokey's nose which she lifted vigorously. That propelled me forward and upward. Gravity worked its inevitable magic and I sailed though the alders into four feet of icy water, with a wild cry and a terrific splash.

I floundered to my feet. Smokey peered down at me through the brush, her ears cocked forward. She nickered inquiringly. I unleashed a torrent of vituperation, the mildest portion of which was, "I'd like to kill you, you no good bitch horse!"

"Don't you dare talk to my horse that way!" It was Becky Ann, her lovely face beside that of her condemned horse. Anger blazed in those beautiful eyes. Standing waist deep in ice water my libido had dried up conversely with my intimate areas getting drenched. I matched anger with anger.

"Well, the hell with you and the horse you rode in on!" I snarled. I said the awful words and couldn't suck them back. The two faces, horsey and lovely, disappeared and as I was clambering out of the stream I heard hoofbeats fading in the distance. She did not leave Smokey for me to ride home on. It was a long hike.

I called Becky Ann, feeling sorrier for myself than for her or her horses. "I'm a jerk..," I began.

"Yes, you are," she said and hung up. Clearly apologizing wasn't going to get it. I sneaked out late that night and stood beneath her darkened second floor bedroom window. I briefly thought of Romeo and Juliet, although I couldn't recall any equine association in that relationship. I needed a lute and a good love song, preferably not "I Ride An Old Paint." But all I found was a handful of pebbles.

I pitched them toward the window and there was an explosive crash as the pane shattered. I ran like hell. No sooner had I dived through my own bedroom window than the phone rang. I scooped it up. "Hello!" I wheezed, out of breath.

"It was you, wasn't it!" she cried, not asking a question.

"First you yell at my horse and then you try to kill me. I don't ever want to see you again!" She slammed the phone down so hard that the concussion stopped up my ear.

"You suppose you could get your friends to call you at a reasonable hour!" my father bellowed from his bedroom. "I'm trying to get some sleep around here."

Life hadn't been this dark for a long time. I'd heard the French Foreign Legion recruited goof offs. Maybe they had a Wisconsin detachment. I really didn't want to go to school the next day and, it turned out, for good reason. Apparently Becky Ann had broadcast my humiliation to everyone. The lovable Scuz Olson, my continuing nemesis, shouted across the school cafeteria, "Hey! It's Duke Wayne! Let's head 'em up and move 'em out, podner! Let's hear them spurs jingle, jangle, jingle!"

Everyone turned and about half of them smirked. I spotted Becky Ann at the center of a group of girls and she was not smirking. She was glowering. My cousin Hal sidled up and whispered, "I hear the ASPCA is after you for horse abuse."

It was a long day.

Even Coach K, who had the sense of humor of a...well, of a goddam horse...offered to make me the manager of the equestrian team.

And then I ran into Debbie Miller and, head down, started to brush past her. She said, "You want a ride home? She looked at me with that sweet, open face and I realized that she'd always been there for me, my best buddy.

"Sure," I said.

"Good," she replied. "I think I have an extra horse."

She might as well have hit me between the eyes with a baseball bat. I fled for the door. I heard her shout, "Wait!" but I banged through the door into the late fall sunshine, taking deep breaths. If my parents said anything about horses I was leaving home. I couldn't believe Debbie had joined the pack.

I grabbed my fly rod and jumped in my rattley old pickup and headed for Thirty Three Creek. I parked at the bridge crossing and headed upstream. There was a pool about a mile in where Debbie and I had taken some big brookies. It was beyond the angler's trail, well past the last bottle cap and gum wrapper. It also was a good place to hunker and sulk. So I moped along with the stream chortling beside me. Whatever the murmuring water was saying, it didn't mention horses and I began to feel better. Not great, just better.

The tannin-rich pool was dark and mysterious, flecks of foam swirling in the grip of the unseen current. I rigged a sinking nymph and flipped it into the pool, counting it down. Then I twitched it back with short pulls. A trout hit hard and the rod bowed. The line hissed through the water. I played the fish to the bank, admired it for a few seconds. A handful of sunsets—that's the way Debbie described the colors of a brook trout and that thought soured me again.

I shook the hook free and the trout, after a moment of disbelief, flipped its tail and vanished.

"Nice fish!" said a voice behind me. I started and whirled and my foot slipped and I lost my balance and fell into the pool with a tremendous splash. I surfaced, sputtering and shivering to see Debbie clutching her sides with helpless laughter.

"Do you do that with every girl you meet?" she wheezed. "Fall into rivers, I mean?" She wiped at her eyes.

"That's right!" I shouted. "Laugh at me like everybody else!" With what dignity I could muster (none), I clambered out of the pool, intending to stalk off.

She jumped in front of me. "Don't you dare run off from me again!" she ordered. "I missed you, you big dope!" She grabbed me enthusiastically and gave me a fierce kiss. I was sopping, she was only less so after squeezing me like a sponge.

I didn't really care and neither did she. "Just don't ever, ever get a horse," I said.

FAST BREAK

Coach K and I had butted heads many times given his antipathy toward humans who didn't wear jock straps. I was, he felt, his cross to bear. I know he was mine.

Coach K and I got crossways from the first day of school my junior year and much of it had to do with the twins, Annette and Janette. That was another sorry episode in my unremitting string of romantic sorry episodes.

Coach K's pyrotechnic temper tantrums made Vince Lombardi look like Ward Cleaver. But rather than being motivational they were merely temper tantrums. He ranted and raved, but rarely offered constructive solutions to the problems that plagued him, like a swarm of yellowjackets.

Coach K had an obsession about the draining effects of girl friends on physical conditioning that bordered on mania. He believed each of us was an incipient sex maniac and that lustful thoughts occupied our minds to the detriment of basketball. That he was right was beside the point. He was equally certain that the high school girls encouraged this priapic preoccupation. In my case he was dead wrong.

He laid it out for us the first day of practice. "I'm Coach Krumhead," he began, whereupon Scuz Olsen snorted a big glob of snot on the gym floor, choked and had to go get a drink of water.

Coach K turned red, white and purple like a chameleon seeking its proper emotional skin tone. Then he roared, "Forty laps after practice, mister! One more outburst like that and you're off the team!"

It was not to be, though. Scuz was the tallest player on the squad and besides he and Coach K shared a revolting sleaziness that made them brothers under their acne-pocked skin. Coach K even tolerated Scuz's rolling thunderous belches in answer to any instructions, as well as his equally revolting other sound effects.

Coach K couldn't help but tolerate Scuz because Scuz had no girl friend. No girl in Birch Lake High, no matter how hard up (Bertha Blomquist, his one-time squeeze, had quit school a year early to work at the Rice Lake creamery as a cheese sorter) could stand him.

"Let's get several things straight," Coach K barked at us as we shifted uncomfortably on the front two rows of the bleachers. He wore an expression that clearly said he considered us human pond scum.

"There's only one boss on this team and I'm it, understand?" We muttered something. "I can't hear you!" he roared.

"Yabba dabba," we muttered louder and he seemed mollified.

"Main thing is women," he said and the word sounded as if he were describing a train wreck. "A basketball player with a girl friend is about as useless as warts on a hammer. He ain't thinkin' back cut; he's thinkin' back seat and I don't want none of it on my team."

"Yabba dabba," we replied, unenthusiastically. None of us was prepared to give up dating for the glory of the Birch Lake Bobcats—especially me for whom dates were as precious as a 14-inch brook trout.

"Okay, let's see what we got here," he said. He divided us into two eight-man squads which was all the boys at Birch

Lake High who could walk and chew gum simultaneously.

The night of our opening game against Edgewater, Coach K sat us on a cold bench in the locker room before we'd had time to get into our uniforms. Kids sat uneasily in their jock straps while the coach stalked among us.

"Boys," said Coach K solemnly, his round face as pasty and ill-formed as the man in the moon. "No matter what happens tonight, I want you to know I'm proud of you." Words he later would eat as if swallowing owl castings.

"You've laid off the girls..." he said.

"Not as much fun as layin' on 'em," whispered Scuz in a voice that could have been heard downtown. Coach K, his rickety train of thought derailed, glared at Scuz.

"Just play our game, work the ball around, get good shots, go for the boards on both ends and play good D." That summary is what every basketball coach has said to every team since the time of Dr. Naismith.

"Okay, let's warm up!" Sounded good to me—my butt was freezing. We finished dressing and spilled onto the court, momentarily addled by the bright lights and the swirling crowd. We broke into two lines for a layup drill. I was at the tail of the line nearest the Edgewater bench and the Edgewater cheerleaders, in cute blue-and-white uniforms, were almost touching our line of shooters.

Two of the four cheerleaders were twins, as identical as new pennies. They were as cute as girls get without being cartoons and I'm sure I looked like Clem Kadiddlehopper as I gawked at them. They smiled simultaneously and it was as if someone had thrown open the door of a smelter. My cousin Hal dug an elbow into my ribs. "Come on, dumbhead. It's your turn."

I fumbled with the ball, dribbled sloppily toward the basket and banged one off the backboard that missed the rim entirely. A concerted groan went up, not from the Birch Lake cheering section...but from the Edgewater girls.

Hal frowned at me and I glanced at the bench. Fortunately Coach K was busy with his clipboard, drawing up plays to ensure victory. None of his diagrams included stick figures to indicate distracting cheerleaders. We went to the locker room for our pregame instructions.

Coach K looked at me with the expression of someone getting ready to clean up a dog's mess on the carpet. "You're starting ball handler," he said. "Forget the cheerleaders—they ain't ours anyway." And I thought he wasn't looking.

Hunk Dayland and Ole Nordland were the forwards, Scuz at center and my cousin Hal at the other guard. Hunk and Ole looked like a pair of oxen and were able to jump at least a half-inch off the floor. Maybe Scuz could intimidate the opposing center by farting at him.

"Okay, boys, this is it," Coach K said. "Let's bow our heads." Geez, I thought, not a prayer.

But that's what it was. And Coach K went right for the spiritual throat: "God, let us win," he implored. "And, Lord, not wishing any harm on the other guys, if anybody has to get hurt let it be them. And let our shots go in and our D be good, in His name we ask it, Amen."

Hunk Dayland, who was a devout Lutheran, remained with his head bowed until Coach K shouted, "Hey, Lunk, you asleep?" It defused the sanctity of the moment as effectively as did the deep aroma of stale sweat in our locker room.

"A-men and A-women!" Scuz exclaimed. "Let's stick it to 'em, Bobcats!" We crowded through the door like the vintage Keystone Kops and burst into the gym to a cheer from the home town crowd. It was a new season, unsullied by loss and untainted by mishap. At least for the first 30 seconds.

As the crowd hushed for the tipoff, the Edgewater pep squad, led by the beautiful twins, shouted, "Yah! Rah! Number Twenty-Four!" I glanced at the man I would be guarding and noticed that he was wearing an odd number. So were all the Edgewater players. We had the even numbers. Who would No. 24 be? The crowd wondered and so did I. I swiftly checked my teammates' numbers around the jump circle and none were wearing that number.

And I realized they all were looking at me. I glanced down to see, upside down, the fateful numbers. "Time out!" Coach K bellowed, although the game had not started. The referee, poised to flip the tipoff, stopped in confusion, blew his whistle by mistake and muttered a foul curse. We trooped to our respective benches.

Coach K looked at me. "Why the hell are they cheering for you?" he snarled. I felt my face pulse hotly.

"I don't know," I mumbled.

"Well, stop it!" he snapped, as if I had any power over girls, especially ones I didn't know.

We started the game in some confusion. Edgewater shouldn't have been much competition for us, but about halfway through the first quarter I brought the ball down the right side, planning to pass to Ole on the corner, who would lob to Scuz, who would drop an in-your-face layup and no doubt say something really obnoxious to the man guarding him. Scuz wasn't a trash talker—more like an offal talker.

"Hi, Cutie!" said a voice beside me as I dribbled along the sideline past the Edgewater cheerleading section. I picked up my dribble, barely avoiding taking steps, and when I glanced at the cute cheerleader a few feet away the kid guarding me neatly stripped the ball and dribbled the length of the floor for a layup.

Coach K's bellowed "Time out you idiot!" probably was audible on the moon. "What the hell's the matter with you?" he snarled at me in the huddle. "You handle the ball like old people pole vault. It's those damn girls isn't it? It's that little Edgewater girl. She was cheering for you, wasn't she?"

The buzzer mercifully stopped Coach K in mid-rant and he realized he had not given us instructions from his bountiful store of basketball lore. "Get out there and...get out there!" he said. "Score more points than they do!" he shouted as we prepared to take the ball out. Thus inspired we went into halftime trailing a bunch of log truck kids by eight points.

As we left the floor, our heads down, our coach fuming and

growling like a dog guarding a bone, they did it again, "Yay! Rah! Number Twenty-Four." I was horribly embarrassed. It seemed that everyone was looking at me, probably because everyone was.

Coach K left me alone for the duration of the halftime break, possibly because he'd given me up as a lost cause. We lined up for the second half tipoff and the ball came to me. In my embarrassed confusion I forgot that we changed goals at the half. I snagged Scuz's tip and broke for the basket, with the crowd yelling what I thought was encouragement.

I laid a neat finger roll...in the wrong basket. I'd scored two points for the Edgewater team. My substitute was waiting at the scorer's table even before the ball hit the floor. "Jesus!" bawled Coach K, and I did not think he was invoking Heavenly intervention again.

We won the game by a few points, though I took no further part in it. "Hey, Coach, you shoulda left him in," Scuz said in the locker room. "He coulda been high scorer for both teams." Coach K was not amused and neither was I.

A week after the game I got a letter which said, "Dear Number Twenty-Four: I am sorry for the dirty trick we played on you. I hope it didn't embarrass you too much. My sister Annette thinks I'm crazy for writing you but I wanted you to know that I'm sorry about cheering for you. Well, that doesn't sound quite right either. Anyway, maybe we'll see each other again. Sincerely, Janette (No. 6)."

That was a really nice thing to do (something I wouldn't have thought of) and I wished there were some way I could thank her for apologizing. But with Debbie in the forefront of my emotional life, and with Edgewater being a competing town it didn't seem right. It was too bad that she wasn't from Birch Lake, able to cheer for me any time she wanted. She couldn't help being from Edgewater. That was a parental flaw.

I wrote, "Hi, Janette, I really appreciate your nice note. It was embarrassing, but kind of nice to have someone cheering for me (our coach isn't known for it). Maybe we can talk sometime if I get up Edgewater way."

Actually, it would not have been a problem to visit Edgewater, 20 miles away. My old pickup truck had made trips longer than that to go fishing. But it didn't seem right to sneak off to Edgewater to see a girl I didn't know when I had one I did know who was supposed to be my steady. There were guys who would do that—Scuz would in a heartbeat—but I would have been ashamed. My heart belonged to Debbie even as my mind said, "You're an idiot."

Basketball season dribbled out, fairly lackluster—we won more games than we lost but other than the Birch Lake weekly no one gave us much ink. I more or less got back in Coach K's good graces (if "good" and "grace" could be used in conjunction with the graceless coach). Mostly it was because he didn't have any alternative. Little guys who could dribble and pass the ball when not distracted were rare in Birch Lake.

We moved into track season and the Tri-County track meet was at Edgewater. The old school had a pocked cinder track where, if you fell, you would acquire bits of cinder in any exposed skin that would linger as black reminders of your high school athletic career well into old age.

Scuz considered himself the natural choice for the hurdle events until he tried the 120-yard highs and not only knocked over every one but also logged the school record slowest time. I had read a book on track technique which put me one up on Scuz who never had read a book of any kind.

I applied the "stepping" approach to hurdling and Coach K observing me in action, sourly said, "You're it." He couldn't resist adding, "Do you suppose you could run them without starting at the finish line and going bassakward?"

I was warming up when I saw the twins, Annette and Janette, across the field. My goosebumps suddenly were not from the cold. They saw me too and one of them waved and began to jog the other direction. The other one did several wind sprints, each of which brought her closer to me.

I guessed the one who ran away was the one who hadn't

bothered to write and the one who was closing in on me was the one who had been kind. Since they were identical it didn't take a force of will to pick one over the other one to like.

"Hey, ain't that one of them girls that you scored the goal for Edgewater for?" Scuz brayed at my elbow. He sniggered and added, "Whyncha give 'er a big slobbery kiss? Maybe she'll let you run on their team?"

My anger flared. I wanted to belt Scuz, but Scuz was known to belt back and he was about a third bigger than me. So I turned on the only feasible target—the twin. "Why don't you leave me alone!" I shouted at who might have been Janette (or maybe not) just as she came within 10 feet of me.

She recoiled as if I'd slapped her. I immediately felt like ten kinds of heel and wanted desperately to apologize, but the presence of Scuz, like the proverbial devil on one shoulder, kept me silent. She turned and walked stiffly off, shoulders hunched as if into a cold wind.

"Boy, you sure told her off," Scuz said. "You got a way with words and with women, I'll give you that." If the measure of my life was that I was standing shoulder to shoulder with Scuz Olsen while a lovely girl who had only wanted to be friends with me, stalked away hurt, it was a fact that I didn't measure up.

"Scuz," I said, "Did anyone ever tell you you're a prick with ears." I brushed by him wondering if there wasn't a race to oblivion on the meet program.

Later, as my first hurdle race neared I spotted the twin alone near the finish line. As far as I could tell I was already finished, but I slunk toward her, looking I'm sure remarkably like an alley mutt sneaking up on someone's unattended hamburger.

"I'm sorry," I mumbled, looking at her track shoes as if they were Cinderella's slippers. "I didn't mean it." She frowned at me curiously, the way someone might study algae flowering on a Petri dish.

"What are you talking about?" she asked.

"I didn't mean to yell at you a while ago," I said. "I was a real jerk."

"It was Janette," she said. "It wasn't me." She thought for a moment and added, "But you were a real jerk."

Great. I couldn't even apologize and get it right. She shook her head and walked away while I mumbled something to the dirty cinders.

They called the high hurdles and I shambled to the starting blocks and settled both into the blocks and in a funk. A second after the starting gun I was at least a step behind everyone else, running as if in a nightmare.

About a third of the way down the 120 yards I lumbered past Coach K who shouted, "My God, old people run faster than that!" I was beginning to weary of being compared to old people by my coach, but had to admit he was right on.

Scuz Olsen bellowed, "Hey, dummy, this ain't a sack race! You're s'posed to use both legs!" Near the finish I glimpsed, through hazed eyes, Annette and Janette, side by side (or perhaps I was seeing double) looking at me as if standing behind yellow crime scene tape.

I stumbled five yards from the finish, went down on my hands and plowed across the finish line on my knees and elbows, shredding skin and embedding bits of cinder. I had kicked over seven hurdles and my time was a tenth of a second slower than Scuz's previous unenviable time.

Coach K with remarkable though accidental prescience said, "You been foolin' with girls again, ain't you?"

There wasn't much of me that didn't hurt, including my pride and my feelings. My various minor injuries added up to enough to keep me from competing any more that day and Coach K, with infinite compassion, said sourly, "We'll try real hard not to miss you."

I limped to the parking lot and sat on the step of the team bus. My self esteem was freckled with cinderlike shards of self-doubt and humiliation. Absently I rubbed at my aching foot, the one that had knocked over seven hurdles.

I sat there until kids started straggling into the parking lot to get on their buses. The Edgewater bus was about 50 feet from me and I watched the twins walk to it, talking to each other. About me, I thought sourly. Wondering how they could rescind a cheer.

They both looked at me. One waved and one turned and climbed on the bus.

What did that mean? Was the wave Janette forgiving me for being a boor or Annette making a derisive gesture. Was the one who didn't wave an angry Janette or an unimpressed Annette? Were there other inhabited planets? Questions with no immediate answer.

As their bus pulled out I saw their faces framed in the rear window, mirror images, looking at me. I waved tentatively and then the bus was gone.

"For God's sake, don't you think about anything else?" It was Coach K, of course. He looked at me as if I were a roadkill and added, "I swear I'm gonna go coach in a monastery."

I stood up painfully and said, "I'm thinking of joining one myself."

He looked narrowly at me. "It figures," he said. "Sure as God made little green apples I'd wind up with you as my ball handler. Brother Bumfuzzle." He gestured at the bus, "Get on. Let's go home."

PLAY A LITTLE SONG

The Starlight was the Birch Lake local dance hall. On Saturday nights the Jack Pine Mellotones filled the northwoods air with polkas and schottisches. The simultaneous stomp of a couple hundred Scanahoovian work boots sounds like rolling thunder: "Dad a dada dad a duh duh...STOMP...dad a dada dad a duh duh...STOMP!"

It was enough to cause war with Sweden.

After a young lifetime of accordions and clarinets I'd had enough of wind-powered instruments. When I was about eight I stumbled onto the Grand Ole Opry on our burly Zenith console radio and was transfixed.

The signal leaped across the country, from Nashville, streaking north through Illinois and into Wisconsin, over the dairy barns and pastures, into the beginning of the North Woods, finally to Birch Lake where it was sometimes scratchy and fading.

Uncle Dave Macon, the Dixie Dewdrop, whaled away at an old banjo and whooped and hollered about his days hauling merchandise in a horse-drawn wagon (this was before my unfortunate experiences with horses).

And Hank Snow, the Singing Ranger (I wondered if he wore

six-guns and carried a badge), played an acoustic guitar, none
of those electric wires trailing from it, and sang about "ma-
mas," those hot-blooded creatures we North Woods kids only
dreamed about.

I lusted to play the guitar—not just play but also sing, just
like Gene Autry. We'd watched the immaculate Gene keep
order on the range when we were little kids. Gene Autry was
the cleanest human being I'd ever seen, his Ipana smile nearly
blinding. Gene could fight four or five black-garbed villains
and never pop a sweat and look as if he'd just stepped out of
the shower into clean clothing. It was miraculous.

Did he ever treat a cow for scours on that ranch of his?
Ever wrestle a powerful calf to the ground to castrate it? I just
couldn't put him in a wrinkled, filthy wool shirt, spattered with
cow shit. In comparison, John Wayne was a hopeless slob who
couldn't sing. But he could and did shoot bad guys dead where
Gene just shot the guns out of their hands and then started
singing—which is when most kids started throwing Milk Duds
and popcorn and yelling at the Birch Lake Rialto screen.

But I liked to hear Gene sing. I would sooner have confessed to consorting with female pigs, but secretly I lusted for a
guitar, not a six gun. I'd pray for the right atmospheric conditions so I'd get a skip from Nashville and the Grand Ole Opry
would come in clear.

I never told anyone I was listening to Hank Williams and
Webb Pierce and Kitty Wells. Every bohunk farm kid was
listening to Frank Sinatra and Joni James. I was learning the
words to Roy Acuff's "Wreck on the Highway."

I met Rusty when Hal and I were playing catch in the flat
behind the station. We always had our gloves and a scuffed
baseball. I caught for the Birch Lake Cookies, our town team,
and Hal played left field. But I wanted to pitch. That was the
glamour position. Who cared about someone squatted behind
the plate wearing padding and a sweat-stained mask that hid
his face and smelled like an old sock?

Rusty Adams had curly, sand-colored hair, a smattering of

freckles and a slightly pugged nose, but not enough to be unat-
tractive. He reminded me of Van Johnson, the movie star. He
was about 23 or so, with a wide grin and he looked like the kind
of fellow a father instantly would trust with his nubile daughter. I looked, I thought, like the kind the father would see and
start searching for a place to hide the kid and then for a dou-
ble-barreled shotgun to protect her. But then I always figured
fathers could read minds.

The two o'clock rumbled through and the engineer waved.
We waved back. "You ever ride a train?" Hal called. He
stretched, checked an imaginary runner, and threw what he
thought was a curve ball. It barely popped in the glove. I
pegged it back out of the crouch.

"Once, with my folks when I was little," I said. "We went
to Minneapolis and I got stomach cramps and pooped in my
pants."

Hal thought he was Bob Feller. He leaned back to put
something extra on the next pitch and heaved a throw six feet
over my head. I flipped the mitt in the air and miraculously
stopped the ball.

Rusty had spotted Hal and me playing catch and had
come over to watch. "You handle the tools of ignorance pretty
well," he said from the shadow of the station house. "Tools
of ignorance...that's what they call catcher's gear." I nodded.
Couldn't have expressed my feelings any better. The new guy
had a soft southern accent.

"Well, I'd rather be a pitcher," I said. "But the coach thinks
I'm a jerk." I didn't add that Coach K thought I was a jerk in
general, not just because I wanted to pitch.

"Lemme show you something," Rusty said. He held out his
hand and Hal flipped him the ball. "Here, see can you catch
this. Be careful." I figured if I could catch Scuz Olsen, the Soo
League burnball king I could catch some rag arm railroad guy.

I set myself for a fast ball, maybe even faster than Scuz's
erratic hummer, but instead I saw the moon, a slow floater that
your Grandma could handle one-handed. It made Scuz's slow-

est pitch look like a screamer. It trundled lazily down the 60 feet between us and I could see the seams—the ball was not rotating.

Then the pitch unaccountably staggered and dropped as if it had hit some invisible obstruction and then it hit me in the crotch, right under my glove. And then I moaned and fell over and lay in the dirt, my lower abdomen trying to turn inside out.

As I scrabbled in the weeds, imitating the dying spasms of a beheaded chicken, my only thought was that I would never be able to discover the intimate delights of girls. I was ruined down there and for the rest of my life. What a terrible thing to do to a teenage virgin!

"Are you okay?" Rusty asked, standing over me. I moaned.

"You'll be okay," he said. "It hurts like hell, but nobody ever broke the family jewels with a knuckleball." Now at least I knew what the lethal weapon was called. The overwhelming ache eased enough that I felt measurably less like vomiting my socks.

"Want to learn how to throw it?" he asked.

"Sure," I groaned, mopping cold sweat off my brow. "There's a lot of people I'd like to castrate."

I found that the knuckleball is a phenomenon that mocks the laws of physics. Some drop, some fade, some do both. Some actually rise. Wind and probably atmospheric conditions influence the diversity and magnitude of the action.

With only five trains a day, Rusty had plenty of spare time to teach me how to throw a knuckleball. Every so often there was some mysterious signal that meant Rusty would have to tap an assortment of clicks on the telegrapher's key. Somehow this meant something to someone and prevented the Soo Line trains from running into each other or off the rails into the remote swamps of the Blue Hills.

But I found that throwing a knuckler was not Rusty's only accomplishment. One day he commented that my fast ball was stinging his hand enough that it would swell and he couldn't finger a G-chord on his guitar.

He was kidding about the fast ball which had all the zip of a baby's patty-cake pat, but I begged him to play something for me. He showed me some simple chords and picking patterns and I was enthralled. He had an old Martin 00-17 guitar, a mahogany-topped little instrument with a voice as mellow as hickory woodsmoke.

The strings cut into my fingertips and the frets buzzed when I tried to hold the chords down. The heel of my hand ached unbearably. "You'll get it. It takes a while to develop calluses," Rusty said. He took the guitar and picked out a bawdy song called "Candyman Blues," and I had him write out the words. I figured that if I couldn't sing "There Stands the Glass" just like Webb Pierce without being laughed out of town, maybe lyrics like "His good sweet candy don't melt away/Just keeps getting' better, so the ladies say..." would hold the audience. Among my crowd it didn't matter how well you sang, it was how dirty the song was.

After I heard Rusty's blues I decided I should have been born a Negro. I bought a guitar for $25 at the Rice Lake hock shop and Rusty said I'd made a good buy. It was an old, simple and worn Gibson flat top, but it had a warm, rich tone and the action was good—low and easy on my fingers.

I was cautious about being seen with a guitar, even by Debbie Miller, my longtime best friend and girl friend. Partly it was because I wanted to surprise her one night with a serenade. Since our dustup over horses and Becky Ann Garner, I was leery of throwing pebbles at the windows of my beloved(s) and figured a guitar might have more impact than a rock, at least emotionally.

"Can you teach me that 'Candyman' thing?" I asked Rusty. Debbie would think I was a man of the world if I sang that beneath her window some night. It never occurred to me what her father might think. He considered me the world's Number One Daughter Molester. He didn't realize I had Debbie so far up on a pedestal that I couldn't have pawed her with my grubby hands if I'd wanted to.

So Rusty showed me a long A-chord and up-the-neck slides and I struggled with it as if I were wrestling a bull calf to earth for castration. Maybe Gene Autry had de-nutted some bull calves after all.

Gradually the guitar submitted and I sounded halfway decent. I practiced behind our cow shed, singing to the heifers, who seemed to enjoy it. My father came home early one day and heard the faint sound of singing and tracked it down. He rounded the corner of the cow shed to behold his only child, his gift to history, his legacy for the future of the world, singing "True Love" to a moon-eyed young female Guernsey cow.

"Jesus H. Christ!" he exclaimed. "What's going on!" And then he hastily added, "Nevermind—I don't want to know."

My mother was more appreciative. "You have a good voice," she said. "It would be nice if you'd sing in church some Sunday."

In front of a crowd! I thought in alarm. Sooner strip buck naked! "They'd laugh!" I said.

"No, they wouldn't," she replied. "They'd love it." I told her I didn't know any hymns and she said that didn't matter. "Just any nice song." "Candyman" clearly was out. As broadminded as the Presbyterians were I suspected that would be a clearcut Sabbath violation. I said I'd think about it. The more I did the more the lure of the greasepaint increased. A captive crowd filled with Christian forgiveness! How could I go wrong even if I went wrong?

One evening Debbie invited me for supper. I was reluctant to break bread with Mr. Miller who always seemed more interested in perhaps breaking some of my more important limbs than he was in breaking bread with me. Mr. Miller was sorry that the practice of castrating males as harem guards and opera singers had gone out of vogue. He considered anyone who looked at his daughter as a candidate for fixing.

He waited until I shoved a fresh baby beet in my mouth, then asked, "You working this summer?" I gnawed frantically at the beet, which slipped around in my mouth like a ball bear-

ing. Beet juice dribbled out of my mouth, giving me the appearance of someone hemorrhaging. Finally I swallowed some
of the sharp little vegetable pieces and croaked, "Don't have a
job. Playing baseball."

"Humph!" he snorted. "Didn't have time for games when I
was your age."

"Oh, Daddy, leave him alone," Debbie said and Mr. Miller
retreated into his cave growling, like a bear with a painful fecal
plug. Mrs. Miller smiled and flustered at me, a mama robin.

"More beets?" she asked. She passed me plates one-by-one,
giving me another as fast as I shuffled the first one along. I
had little time to eat—too busy refusing further helpings. She
seemed worried that I would not like her cooking or perhaps
that I was not getting enough to eat at home.

"You'd better have some more meat," she said, passing another plate. "You barely took any. Is it all right?" I tried to nod
yes and no at the same time—yes, the meat was all right and,
no, I didn't want any more. My head bobbled like one of those
obnoxious rear car window animals. Mr. Miller glowered at me.
Mrs. Miller fluttered. Debbie ate steadily, like a longshoreman,
great heaps of food. I was awed at her capacity for food. Where
did she put it and why didn't it add an ounce to her trim figure?

She was intent on her eating, studying the array of food on
her plate as if it were a scientific experiment, fork poised. I'd
never seen anyone eat with such fierce concentration.

We went to one of the rare movies at the Rialto that didn't
feature John Wayne and afterwards Debbie ate a cheeseburger
and fries at Bamburger's and topped it off with a chocolate sun-
dae. I was awestruck and wondered about my ability to feed
her if we got married, which was the unspoken likelihood of our
relationship.

I continued to visit Rusty at the railroad station and when
we weren't working on my knuckle ball we were working on
guitar chords, especially the seventh of the F-position, a great,
sprawling thing like a spider on the fretboard. I finally managed to grab a few of the six possible notes. "Let the rest go,"

Rusty said. "What the hell, you don't need all those notes anyway."

He hired me as his assistant (I now could tell Mr. Miller that I did have a job, although I doubted it would change his opinion of me as a slavering pervert). It was an arrangement that I don't think the Soo Line knew anything about. Rusty paid me fifty cents an hour and my major duty was to run up the street to Bamburger's to get him Cokes—either that or playing catch or listening to him play guitar.

When Rusty and I weren't maiming each other with knuckleballs we were wrestling with chords. I didn't know which one hurt more. But I had a couple of songs pretty well worked out, including Hank Williams' "Lovesick Blues" which seemed appropriate for Debbie.

One night, after I'd gotten the key of C pretty well subdued I decided to serenade Debbie. The song involved yodeling which, in the ebbtide of adolescence, sometimes surfaced without warning.

The night was soft and sweet, a hint of the lake in the air. The clunk and clatter of the veneer mill was barely audible, almost a rhythm section. A screen door creaked and banged somewhere down the street and a dog barked a couple of times. The moon had been bitten into, but still gave enough light for me to see without a flashlight. I hauled my guitar case into Debbie's yard and quietly unsnapped it, removed the old Gibson and took a deep breath.

I cleared my throat. It sounded like a dump truck unloading in the silent night and I figured Mr. Miller was even at that moment calling the town constable. My romantic balladeering seemed less and less like a good idea. But I was there, I had the guitar in hand, and I figured in for a penny, in for a pound.

Debbie's window was on the second floor, a dozen feet above me. It was open and as I began to sing I saw the curtain pulled aside by a dark shape. My love was listening.

"I gotta feelin' called the blue-hoo-hoos, ah Lawdy!" I quavered, trying to emulate the Hank Williams sound, that of a

sawmill blade cutting through a license plate that was embed-
ded in a log. As I sang I gained confidence and even tried a
single string run or two on the guitar. Why, the Grand Old
Opry was just down the road from Birch Lake—next stop on
my journey through life.

I finished and there was a faint patter of applause from
unseen hands above. Then Mrs. Miller's voice floated down,
like the contents of a chamber pot emptied over a passer-by on
a cobbled Elizabethan street. "That was very nice," she said.
"But Debbie's sleeping over at Melody's house. You'd better
leave before Mr. Miller wakes up. He doesn't like to be dis-
turbed in the middle of the night."

"I'm sorry!" I squeaked, sounding exactly like Mickey
Mouse.

"No one every serenaded me before," Mrs. Miller whispered.
"Mr. Miller doesn't believe in things like that."

"Good bye!" I croaked, stumbling toward the street as if my
pants were down around my ankles, clutching my guitar case
with a sweaty hand. I wondered if Juliet's mom ever shouted
down to Romeo, "Hey, kid, nice song but my husband's gonna
rip your throat out."

A couple of weeks later my mother told my grandmother
about the possibility I would sing in church and my grandmother ordered me to do it. She asked, actually, but an ask from my
grandmother was equivalent to a direct order from Gen. George
Patton.

I had the sheet music for "Dear Hearts and Gentle People, a
Meredith Willson tune. I figured I could fumble through most
of the chords and keep the congregation from charging the
pulpit like a Mongol horde. After all how tough could it be to
entertain a bunch of bored Presbyterians, some of whom had
Bruenig's Lager hangovers from Saturday night at the Bluegill
Bar.

Some also were marking time until they could go fishing.
But their wives would keep them in line long enough for me to
stagger through "Dear Hearts," satisfy my mother and grand-

mother, and get back to the heifers who always appreciated my balladry.

My confidence lasted only until I sat down in church and the reality of being there and the looming fact that I would have to face an audience turned me to tapioca. The church was hot. A few somnolent wasps bumbled drunkenly into the windows and clung to the walls.

I sat in the front row, clutching my guitar by the neck as if it were a dead turkey. My palms were cold with sweat and I wiped them on my pants. I couldn't imagine how I had let myself get into this.

The minister introduced me as if I were Frank Sinatra. "... will sing for you now." He looked expectantly at me and I realized that my time had come. I knew how Death Row inmates felt when the guards open the cell door and say, "It's time, Lefty."

I stumbled up the two steps to the podium and looked out at the congregation. Was it my imagination or were they all snarling and frothing at the mouth? Every eye was fixed on me. There is nothing more frightening than the first time in front of a crowd, the awful hush of anticipation and the terrible certainty that no matter how low their expectations you won't come within howitzer range of them.

Rusty had told me, "Just imagine they're all buck-naked." But when I tried that I was horrified. Mrs. Windmiller was a wrinkled bag of skin, a 200-pound woman who had shrunk over the years to half that. She looked like she should be tracking escaped convicts with her nose to the ground.

I strummed an introductory chord and then couldn't remember the first words to the song until I realized there were the same as the title and I croaked into it. I was off-key, my voice quavering. The guitar buzzed and thunked because I couldn't hit the strings accurately. I rushed the lyrics, hoping to end this horror as quickly as possible. My legs were weak. I felt I might just topple over. I couldn't get enough breath and teetered on the brink of hyperventilation.

Old Mrs. DeHaven fell asleep in the front pew and began to snore. Her neighbor poked her with an elbow and the old lady started awake and shouted, "Praise God!" and then looked around in confusion. I sang grimly on, this never-ending song that no one wanted to hear.

Then, in the middle of "...who live and love in my home town...." spit leaked down my throat and I swallowed involuntarily and my throat painfully locked. At that instant a wasp lost its grip and tumbled off the wall behind me, did a lazy somersault and landed on the back of my neck. Apparently it blamed me for its clumsiness because it instantly stung me.

Those dear hearts and gentle people then were shocked to hear me shout, "Ow! Shit fuck! God damn!"

The minister who had seen what happened, reacted as only a true Christian would. He applauded my song, encouraged the congregation to do likewise, and thanked me profusely for sharing my talent with everyone. So quickly did he react that most folks thought they hadn't heard right and forgot about it. As I slunk back to my pew he caught my eye and winked. Bless his heart, it was enough to make a churchgoer out of me.

My mother invented the laser beam right on the spot, years before anyone else. Her glare would have bored holes in sheet metal. I managed to slip out of the church the instant the service ended and before she could corral me.

Rusty whooped when I told him what had happened and said, "Must be some pretty good ol' boys ministerin' up here. You do something like that down home and them ol' Baptist preacher boys'd lock your soul up in Hell before you got the last bad word out."

"I was so damn scared to sing in front of everyone," I said.

"Everybody is the first time," he said. "It's like sex—you get better at it."

"I wouldn't know," I said. We picked up our ball gloves and threw knuckle balls for an hour. My mother weakened some when she saw the big red knot on the back of my neck, but did mutter, "That's nothing to what Jesus suffered on the cross and you didn't hear him cursing the Lord," as she applied baking soda to sooth the pain. Wisely I kept my mouth shut.

Rusty got his draft notice two days later. He had 30 days to report. "Probably wind up in Korea," he said. "I ain't lookin' forward to that."

Nor would I—North Koreans never had bothered me and I'd never bothered them. It seemed like a good arrangement. But I still had most of two years of high school to worry about the draft. Rusty wasn't that lucky.

I saw him later on the day he got his notice, up near the Village Hall. He was staring at the memorial to Birch Lake's war dead, going back all the way to the Civil War. It was an obelisk with the names of those who had died in the various wars but had not been updated to Korea...yet. He didn't see me and when I realized what he was looking at I turned and went the other way.

Rusty wrote me a couple of times from basic training. He'd found another Mississippi boy who played harmonica and they were making music together. He sounded happy, but said he didn't care for the rigorous training and the structured hours. "I'm used to being my own boss," he wrote. "Kind of tough to get ordered around by everyone. Maybe they'll make me an officer and I can do the ordering. Watch out for flying pigs—if you see any you'll know that happened."

The second letter was just before he shipped out for Korea. His harmonica-playing buddy had gone on ahead and he'd put the little Martin away for safekeeping. "Don't think there'll be much time or place to pick any music over there," he said. "I'll store my little sweetheart until I get home and then you and me will make some good sounds together."

I got one letter from Korea which said it was quiet most of the time but you never knew. He didn't talk about music or baseball, just about the uncertainty.

Months went by with no word.

Then the new station agent, a florid, middle-aged man with a sour disposition, called to say I had a box at the depot and would I come get it—this said in a tone that implied he had notified me a dozen times already and had been ignored. I doubted I would learn any new pitches or chords from him, just how to be unpleasant.

I hurried down to the station and signed for the box. Rusty's name was atop the return address. I didn't want to open the package in the presence of the glowering station agent and awkwardly tucked it under my arm and raced home.

I ripped the top off the big cardboard box. There was a guitar case inside with letter taped to the top. I slid the case out and opened it. It as Rusty's little Martin guitar. I looked at it confused and then remembered the letter and tore it open.

"I guess you're wondering why I'm sending you my guitar," the letter began. "Well, I had a little accident over in Korea. Stuck my left hand in front of a mortar shell and got it blowed off. Kind of hard to finger a D-chord with a stump.

"The docs say I can get one of those artificial hands with a hook and be pretty normal, but none of them play guitar. Guess I'll have to take up the mouth harp.

"Anyway, I wanted you to have my little girl because I know you appreciate her. Write me sometimes and let me know how you and my sweetheart are getting along. Hope you have a good life and keep throwing that knuckler.

"Your friend, Rusty."

My father came in from work just as I finished the letter. He took in the packing case and the guitar in my lap and frowned as he started to say something. I held the letter out to him and he took it and read it.

When he finished we looked at each other and then he did something he hadn't done for a long time. He put his arm around me and I bawled into his shoulder.

Some time later I went out behind the cow shed with the little Martin and I sang "Candyman Blues" to the heifers.

THE EXTERNAL FLAME

My Uncle Al had resisted the lure of romance for more than 50 years. He was content with the company of females only if they were hairy, loped on four legs and retrieved ducks. Women were creatures from another planet, to be avoided because they might have the power of death rays. And most of them considered Bruenig's Lager as Devil urine, which showed they had no appreciation for the finer things in life.

And then he encountered Amanda Soderberg, 250 pounds of Scandinavian flesh. She had the comfort of a Warm Morning cook stove on a cold winter day. She radiated love like the stove radiated heat and she promised with her very presence to bake your biscuits good and brown.

Uncle Al had been my fishing buddy since I was 12 years old—old enough to know what sin was , but not old enough to do much about it. Uncle Al, on the other hand, had decades of experience in the hellholes of life. His vice mostly was Bruenig's Lager, but he had been in the Army in World War One and often implied exciting times in Paris until my Grandmother shut him up with a look that would melt titanium. My grandmother was old school and still treated the 50-year-old Al as if he were 13 and hapless.

Uncle Al was hapless, but grizzled and toothless (he had

false teeth, but they were perpetually misplaced). He hunted and he fished and kept the family in wild sustenance.

Uncle Al and Amanda found each other at the Bluegill Bar where Uncle Al was keeping the Bruenig Brewery in business. "Good beer," she said, nodding at the platoon of empties on Uncle Al's table. He gawped. No one he knew considered Bruenig's "good." "Cheap," yes...but good? And a woman, no less.

Without invitation (which would have come only if a meteorite the size of Birch Lake was a half-mile from impact on the Bluegill Bar), she plopped down in a chair across the table from Uncle Al and said, "I'm Amanda Soderberg. I been cookin' out at the Lake Point Resort for a couple of months but thought I'd come in and see what the night life in Birch Lake is all about." Uncle Al was speechless. It was as if one of his Labs had started talking.

"Don't say much do you? I like a guy like that." Absently she picked up a damp empty and scratched through the label with her thumbnail, separating it into two pieces. "Heard a guy say once if you could do that you're a sex machine. What's your name?"

Uncle Al looked to God for inspiration but of course that wasn't going to happen and he finally choked out, "Al!" "Well, Al," she said, "How about I buy us a beer each?" Uncle Al had never been known to turn down a free beer and he wasn't about to start, even if his benefactor was a woman.

And what a woman! She jiggled even when sitting. She was fat, sure, but mostly big-boned and big hearted. She was Love personified. Uncle Al had met the irresistible force, the love machine that turned him from a grumpy, grizzled old reprobate into a love baby, all giggly and squirmy. It was downright disgusting.

I fell under her spell a couple days later when I went into the Bluegill looking for Uncle Al and he introduced me as his favorite nephew and fishing buddy. It was astonishing enough to see him sitting at a table with a woman, apparently not tied down with steel cable or without his leg in a bear trap, but he was practically simpering as he looked at her. This could not be my Uncle Al, the man whom I revered because he lived his life like a Jack London character and didn't need anything except a fishing rod and a shotgun.

Certainly not a woman, especially one who looked like a cross between Marilyn Monroe and a Green Bay Packer pulling guard.

"My Gawd!" Amanda squealed, "He's a cute little bugger ain't he!" And she grabbed me in a bear hug that was like being assaulted by a featherbed. There were billowy breasts and huge arms and thunder thighs all over me. This wasn't a woman—this was a force of Nature. She released me and I staggered back, breathing hard and blushing. "By Gawd, if you was a couple years older I'd drag you home with me!" she roared. A sheen of beer sweat coated her red face and she beamed like Oliver Hardy in the middle of a scam.

I had to admit Amanda was a long way from ugly in the face. But if Uncle Al wanted the kind of girl that I went to movies to see, he needed to run her in the Tri-County Marathon, maybe a couple of times, and shave a couple hundred pounds off her.

Was I jealous? You bet. She was stealing my fishing buddy and I didn't want to be part of an extended family. I wanted Uncle Al to myself, just me and him on Birch Lake, maybe up toward the Narrows where the walleyes hung out.

Uncle Al drove no motor larger than five horsepower—his trusty Johnson outboard—but Amanda had a rusty 1949 DeSoto pickup and I would see them tooling around Birch Lake. God knows where they went, but it wasn't fishing. Amanda squealed in revulsion when I showed Uncle Al a Prince Albert canful of leeches I'd collected for walleye bait. A woman who couldn't stand to be around leeches was a woman to be wary of.

This epic love affair began to come unraveled when the Rev. Willard Humspeak came to town with his Holy Word of God Revival. It was the second time a revivalist had come to Birch Lake and I well remembered the last time, the run-in with

Brother Snyder and Flame LaTouche. I figured no good could come from a revival except to revive some bitter experiences.

Brother Willard was almost a clone of Brother Snyder. Apparently they had some sort of preacher machine in the South that stamped these guys out of the same raw material and sent them north to convert Bruenig's Lager drinkers. Certainly there was plenty of opportunity in Birch Lake.

Birch Lakers felt they were not in need of salvation. To a person they figured they either had earned their Heavenly stripes or it was too late. But there was something about the good Brother Willard as there is about any evangelist that drew them to his ragged tent. Most of it was the lack of entertainment in Birch Lake. And he played pretty good guitar and sang what would have been rock and roll except the name of Jesus was omnipresent.

We weren't likely to get Fats Domino at the Bluegill Bar; Brother Humspeak was next best in his Word of God tent. It was the guitar that pulled me into the back of the tent. If I couldn't have Fats or B.B. King, I'd take what I could get.

Brother Willard looked remarkably like Elvis Presley, complete with black sideburns and a pelvic twist for Jesus as he belted out "Take Me As I Am." I found myself swaying with what might have been God's spirit entering my soul, but then I did the same thing with Little Richard singing "Good Golly, Miss Molly" on the jukebox at the Bluegill Bar.

To my disappointment Brother Willard put down his guitar after a rousing rendition of "Glory Be To Jesus" and began to speak. "I tell you, good folks, you live in God's paradise..." he said in a low baritone, breathing into the microphone like he was making a dirty phone call. We knew it was paradise, God's or otherwise, but it was nice to hear someone from outside validate our opinion. "The lakes and the trees and the good sunshine, they're all God's handiwork."

I actually heard someone murmur "Amen," but it must have been a tourist from down South—maybe Milwaukee or Madison. We loved the lakes and the trees and the sunshine, but we weren't about to turn it into a religious experience. "Pick the guitar," I whispered, but he continued, his voice rising and becoming hoarse, although he'd only been talking for a few moments.

"And I say unto you, brothers and sisters, there is sin among these lakes and trees and under this sunshine. Sin!" Son of a gun—I was missing the whole thing. Sin here and none of it mine.

I noticed there was an uncommon preponderance of women in the audience, especially in the first three rows of folding chairs. Most were well-fed, like Amanda, and they cooled themselves with fans from the Swenson Funeral Home and soaked up redemption. Brother Willard seemed to be speaking directly to them, ignoring the scattering of men in the back, all of whom harbored sins of one kind or another—taking the name of the Lord in vain was an almost momentary occurrence in their lives.

"Can't you feel the power?" he asked. "Can't you just feel the power of the Lord a-creepin' into your bones! Movin' up your earthly body like the hot fire of Heaven!" More than one woman was squirming and I couldn't tell if it was Heaven fire or chiggers.

Brother Willard had reached a fever pitch when a black Labrador belonging to the owner of the pasture where Brother Willard had erected his tent wandered onto the stage behind Brother Willard and lifted his leg to the guitar which rested against the amplifier. There was a blinding flash of light and the Lab flew halfway across the stage, yowled in pain and fright and disappeared into the night.

Without missing a beat Brother Willard roared, "Begone, black devil! Into the night from whence you came! And thus Jesus casts out the devils in us all and makes us whole!" He went on from there, while I mourned the smouldering Gibson guitar. But you had to admire the good reverend's adaptability.

The audience broke into cheers and a huge shape rose from the semi-darkness at the side of the tent and shouted,

"Amen, Brother!" It was Amanda and my mouth dropped open. Amanda, the beer-drinking waitress girl friend of my Uncle Al. She was transformed into an Angel of Redemption by a pissing Labrador retriever. Conversion comes in strange ways.

From that moment she was a changed person and she in turn tried to change my Uncle Al, mostly by inveigling him into attending a revival meeting with her. Talk about a test of love! Uncle Al in any form of church was as unthinkable as him switching to another brand of beer. But I reckoned without the power of whatever hormonal imperative had Uncle Al by his testicles.

"But, Honeybuns, you gotta go!" Amanda boomed and Uncle Al winced as if a bullet had just missed his ear. Uncle Al had been called many things, but "Honeybuns" was not one of them. "It'll change your life." I was pretty sure Uncle Al had no desire to have his life changed, but I could see him weakening under the steady barrage of love radiating from his plush companion. It was sickening to see, like watching a lovely old barn collapse in a strong wind.

I'd just about given up fishing with Uncle Al while That Woman was around, but he asked me to go with him one Saturday afternoon. Uncle Al and I sat in the gently bobbing green rowboat that he had dubbed "The Birch Lake Bitch." His antique Johnson outboard clung to the transom and we were anchored off Snake Island, casting to the weedbeds for pike. He was 140 pounds of whang leather, as wind and sun cured as a salmon steak.

"Where's Amanda?" I asked.

"Meetin' with that preacher man," he said. "He's been tryin' to talk her into getting' saved and she's been tryin' to talk me into it too. Says she'll do it if I will."

"I don't know what 'getting saved' means," I said.

"Me neither," Uncle Al said, popping the cap on a bottle of Bruenig's. "But there's a lot of hollerin' and o-Jesusin' and they all seem to get worked up about it. I ain't gonna do it."

"What if Amanda makes you do it?" I asked. Uncle Al was

silent for a long time, his gnarly fingers curled around the
bottle of beer. He shook his head, like a horse beleaguered by
flies.

"Bobby, I'm nuthin' but uh feather in the wind," he said, an
observation which was as confusing as it was unexpected. He
put the beer down and picked up a lure.

"Feather in the wind," he repeated to the Dardevle he was
snapping to his line. I knew it had something to do with Amanda (his statement, not the lure), but being a callow teenager
has some advantages—you don't know what to say to something like that, but you aren't expected to know either. So I
cast my Pikie Minnow and had a hit from a three-pound snake
pike and we forgot about it, whatever It was.

Uncle Al's infatuation continued undiminished, but Amanda
began to spend more time with Brother Willard, learning, I
guess, the ways of the Lord and being redeemed. Sometimes
she was so redeemed she was out of breath when she reap-
peared at the Bluegill Bar and ordered a depth charge—a
change from Bruenig's to something far more challenging.

Uncle Al pouted, a terrible sight, but she threw a meaty
arm around his bony shoulders and said, "Oh, Al, don't get so
fussy! You come to the meeting tonight and I'll love you forever."

Uncle Al muttered something about "when Hell freezes
over" and Amanda said, "I'm gonna freeze you over if you don't
do this one little thing for me."

I sat nursing a Coke and silently pleaded with Uncle Al to
return to himself, rowdy, dirty, unkempt and totally lovable.
But he squirmed like a little kid and finally agreed to go to the
meeting.

"Oh, you'll just love Brother Willard!" she exclaimed and I
thought to myself, not like you do. I had dark suspicions about
Amanda's relationship with the good shepherd, figuring her
for a great big ol' sheep to his randy crook. Uncle Al may have
known every shady dodge when it came to hunting and fishing,
but he was as innocent as baby sweat when it came to women.

Oh, Uncle Al, I thought, what have you gotten into! I'll bet you wouldn't know a walleye from a feedlot hog.

I had not heard the term "pussy whipped" at that time, but years later when I did I immediately thought back to that moment. If she asked him to ride a horse, I'll bet he'd do that too, I thought wryly. Fortunately there wasn't a horse in Birch Lake big enough for Amanda.

So, horses were out...but the revival was in. I tagged along behind them as they entered the revival tent that night. I hovered in the background where the strung lights didn't reach and listened to Brother Willard whip up the crowd. He had rewired the Gibson and with a wary eye out for incontinent Labradors, he entertained the crowd with a couple of lively gospel numbers.

His speakers had been damaged somewhat and the effect was a Jimi Hendrix fuzz guitar several years before Hendrix came on the scene. All he needed to do was play the National Anthem and set his guitar on fire.

Then it was time to proselyte and he was good at it. I even felt the spirit stirring in me, although it might have been indigestion from the double cheeseburger I'd had at Bamburger's earlier.

"Those who will be saved! Come forward NOW!" shouted Brother Willard at the penultimate moment of his peroration. The crowd swayed and moaned, caught in the throes of religious fervor, and several stood and began to move toward the low stage where Brother Willard stood ready to lay on hands.

Then Amanda was on her feet, dragging a shapeless bundle I recognized as my Uncle Al to his feet behind her.

Amanda marched to the stage like a Sherman tank, with Uncle Al, a spavined Jeep, trailing behind her. He looked as if he were going to the gallows.

She stood in front of the good brother, hands clasped to her bounteous bosom, while Uncle Al hid in a semi-crouch behind her, looking as miserable as a cat taking a bath. "Oh, ye shall be saved!" bellowed Brother Willard and he thrust a healing hand at Amanda with results never anticipated in the Halls of Heaven.

He had intended to give her a healing palm on the forehead but instead it was a hefty dope slap that rocked her backward on her rounded heels. The effect was like swatting a punching dummy, the kind that no matter how hard you hit it, it bounces back up. Crying, "Oh, Lord, I am saved!" she threw up her hands, lost her balance and fell backward like a 300-year old redwood.

Uncle Al looked up from his reverential pose, warned by a shadow that, given the circumstances, could have signaled the approach of an angel. He had but a nanosecond to ponder this before 257 pounds of sweating Amanda engulfed him.

They crashed to the floor together, the romance shattering along with Uncle Al's left femur. Uncle Al suffered both a broken leg and a broken heart. She bounced up, ignoring my writhing uncle behind her, and clutched Brother Willard by the knees, sobbing, "Take my love, Brother Willard, take me!" He looked the way a frog does when a snake has its hindquarters swallowed and is working its way up the body—resigned, but somehow relieved that the trials of life are ending.

Amanda continued to attend the revival sessions while Uncle Al languished on the front porch, a Bruenig's in hand. Brother Willard left town at the end of his camp meeting and Amanda disappeared at about the same time. Maybe they ran off together to experience The Rapture.

I stopped by to see how Uncle Al was doing. He hadn't shaved for a couple of days and his false teeth were removed. He gave me a huge grin that was like looking into a bat cave, and said, "Hey, boy, you think you're big enough to run that Johnson outboard?"

I nodded. He said, "Let's go catch us some Paradise."

CHARLIE PETE

It's no wonder my mother's brow took on heavy worry lines when I told her I was heading to the Brule to go fishing. I was too old for her to forbid such nonsense, but too young (in her view) to be doing such a thing, given my past experience up to and including the blasphemous morning in church.

Since the minister obviously had forgiven my wasp-inspired blasphemy mother could do no less than the same, although her inclination was to ground me for life.

I figured it would be wise to get out of town quickly, before she left the house and immediately ran into neighbors, friends and even strangers who would commiserate with her about having a kid who not only couldn't sing, but trashed the Lord's manor in a dramatic way.

Fortunately my father had gone fishing on Spider Lake and knew nothing of the Holy Hootnanny. If I were lucky I could enlist in the Foreign Legion somewhere between Birch Lake and Hayward and come home only after things cooled down.

Five miles out of town I saw Charlie Pete walking along the road. He appeared to be sober—at least he wasn't weaving. He was a pretty good old boy when he wasn't drunk. Actually he was a pretty good old boy drunk too, but hard to communicate with. Charlie was a Chippewa Indian or Ojibway if you preferred that name.

I stopped and hollered at him, "Hey, Charlie, you want a ride?"

"You goin'?" he said. I assumed he meant "Where are you going?" not inquiring as to whether I was mobile.

"Up to the Brule," I said.

He gimped over to the truck and climbed in beside me. There was a whiff of old booze and old sweat, but he wasn't too bad. "How's your grandma?" he asked. "She's a pretty good ol' lady."

Charlie did odd jobs around town in the daytime and got drunk at night. My grandma had known the Pete family forever. Her parents had come overland from Ohio in a covered wagon and first cooked for the log crews and then opened a restaurant.

"She's good," I said. "She tells me about the old days and that's pretty interesting stuff. In fact she was telling me about your daddy the other night. We were out on the porch. You know, the night the thunderstorm blew up?" Charlie grunted.

My grandmother loved to tell stories about her younger days and most of the family tuned her out, but I was fascinated by them. When she told about Charlie's father and the things he had done when she was a girl, I pictured an Indian somewhere between Crazy Horse and Superman.

"Your daddy must have been a heck of a guy," I said to Charlie and he shrugged. "Once," he said. "But then he got old and just laid down one night and died."

That wasn't the way my grandmother remembered Lloyd Pete. "He and my father were the strongest two men I ever knew," she said that night on the porch, with the katydids rasping and the hum of the mill in the distance. I could smell the lake, a rich scent of green and blue.

"My father was a big gruff man who smelled like fresh sawdust and pipe tobacco and my mother always smelled of fresh-baked bread," my grandma said. "They were soft and comforting smells in a hard life. In those days you either were a logger or an Indian," she said. "Logging was an awful way to make a living. If a falling tree didn't kill you, you could fall in the river during a log drive and drown. Most loggers couldn't swim and if they fell they died.

"The Indians were wearing white man's clothing by then— that was about 1900. They lived on the reservation but they'd float down the chain of lakes in canoes and pole through the rice beds, knocking the rice into the canoes until they floated so low in the water that you'd wonder why they didn't sink.

"They'd camp right below our house on the riverbank. We children would see the flickering lights of their campfires at night and wonder what they were doing." My grandmother stopped and rocked in the summer evening and I heard the faint chugging of machinery at the veneer mill on the lake.

"The only Indian I ever knew well then was Lloyd Pete, the father of Charlie Pete, that poor man who gets drunk all the time. I was in the cafeteria when a huge old man with a limp came in and acted crazy. He was big and strong and his hair hadn't been cut in a long while. He began to rant about Indi- ans and I think he may have been mean drunk. He said his family had been killed by the Sioux in the Minnesota uprising back in the 1860s when he was a boy.

"He said four Sioux came to the house and demanded liquor from his mother. When she wouldn't give them any they shot her and then clubbed his little sister to death. They set fire to the cabin and when the father came running from the field they shot him too."

We were shocked. "Was this true?" my mother asked.

My grandmother shrugged. "I don't know, but it made a good story and scared me. I was only fourteen, after all." She paused and rocked some more. "He said his limp came from a wound he got fighting the Sioux with General Custer. He said the wound kept him from going on the march that ended at the Little Big Horn. That was really only a few years from when that massacre happened.

"And it was only a few years from when the soldiers killed so many Indians at Wounded Knee in South Dakota. The man said he was sorry he hadn't been there to kill Indian women and children. He was a frightening old man and he was filled with hate for whatever reason.

"And then Lloyd Pete came in to buy some day-old bread which my mother always saved for him. He was a wonderful man, a kind of mystic to the other Indians. They called him a shaman and they thought he could work magic.

"But when he walked in all that awful man could see was an Indian. He began to curse Lloyd Pete. Called him a killer of little children. Lloyd Pete looked exactly to me anyway like a picture I'd seen of Sitting Bull with his broad, seamed old face. I was only fourteen years old, but I realized that you can't judge by appearance. The white man was nasty and bad and Lloyd Pete was good...but he looked like someone they'd sent an entire army to kill.

"Lloyd Pete didn't say a word. He just picked up his bread and started to leave. The man shouted at my mother and slammed his cane on the counter. He clenched his fist and looked as if he was going to hit her for giving bread to an Indian. Before he could move Lloyd Pete had picked him up and threw him right through the front window. Took the frame, glass and all, right out across the board sidewalk and into the muddy street.

"The man rooted into it just like a boar hog. Lloyd Pete turned to my mother and said, 'I'm sorry, ma'am. I'll fix the window.' And he did too. He bought the materials and built the window all new."

I thought of that story and glanced over at Charlie Pete who rocked and bobbed with the motion of the truck as it jounced over potholes in the road. He was grizzled and dirty and did not look like a noble savage or a noble anything else.

"Charlie, my grandma told me a story about the time your daddy threw a guy through the window of my grandma's restaurant. You know anything about that?"

"Daddy could do 'most anything," Charlie said. "He could pass spells I think. They said one time a white man picked a fight and knocked him down. Daddy just looked at the man for a long time and that night the man was heading home on his horse and he was struck by lightning."

"Geez!" I said. "You think your daddy did that?"

Charlie shook his head. "He was a medicine man and he knew how to live off the land. He knew how to find deer in the winter when folks got hungry, but there was one winter that was the worst I ever seen around here. We all just about starved—a few old ones did.

"They came to my daddy for help and he built a shake lodge and talked to the spirits. Seemed like it always worked before but it didn't that time. People stayed hungry and your grand-ma gave away a lot of food to keep folks from starving. Seemed like the fire went out of daddy after that and he was just an-other Indian."

I looked at Charlie. He was looking out the window at the tree-lined road as if he were watching his history pass by. "You can let me out up at the Lake Road," he said. "I can walk on down to the house from there."

It was at least a mile from the blacktop to his ramshackle house by Long Lake. "I'm not in any hurry," I said. "I'll take you home." I swung onto the gravel road. "So what happened to your daddy?" I asked.

Charlie shrugged. "He died." There was a long pause and then Charlie said. "He's buried right up ahead. You ever see a grave house?" I shook my head. "Stop up by that big pine and I'll show you," he said.

I hadn't bargained on visiting an Indian burial site, but didn't want to hurt his feelings, so I pulled over and we got out. "It's right back in here," Charlie said, gimping across the road ditch and over the berm. He pushed aside a low-hanging bough and I followed him.

We came to a sunlit clearing where there was a little almost collapsed structure, about eight feet long and a couple of feet high. "That's a grave house," Charlie said. "My daddy's buried there." The grass around it was rank and the wood was rotted and gray.

"I found daddy dead," Charlie said. "He just up and died. I guess he didn't have nothin' to live for after his magic went away. My momma found a shaman up on the reservation and he told us how to give my daddy an Indian funeral.

"Like yesterday I can hear that old man talkin' to my momma. I was only eight, but nothin' like that ever happened before. 'Wash the body,' he told her. 'He needs to be clean when he goes to where the spirits live.'"

Charlie wasn't looking at me and I don't think he was look-ing at the grave either. He was looking at the past. He became what he once was and I might as well have been someplace else. He surely was. "Make your faces black," he said, not to me, but to an assembled family in memory. He was the sha-man, not Charlie and my mouth felt dry. "Wait for the fourth sun," he said. "He must be buried in his best clothing and with his mide bag, his magic. When you have wrapped him in birch bark I will come and perform the ceremony. I know of him and his magic. He was one of the last of us. I will help him on his way. It is the least I can do for my brother."

This was scary—an old drunk Indian somehow had become, at least in his mind, an Ojibway shaman from a half century before. Shadows from the overhead trees danced on the grave house as a breeze riffled the treetops. Charlie looked at me and he was Charlie again. "That old shaman smelled like a goat and his nose run," Charlie said. "But he had that magic like my daddy did and we all knew he was a magic man and could do magic things."

Charlie shook his head, retreated once again to another time. "This spot was more open then. A lot of these trees growed up since we buried Daddy. That grave house was new wood too. I oughta do somethin' to fix it up. Probably won't.

"'My dear friends....' That's the way the old shaman started out. 'I'm not family to this man except we share the blood and

the bone of the Ojibway and that makes us brothers. I speak
for him as if I was his family. He has gone where the deer
always yard close by and the fish never fail to darken the shallows. Don't be sad. Just know we'll be together in this happy
land someday.'"

Charlie hobbled to the grave house and bent over stiffly and
pulled a couple of weeds. "The old shaman brought along a
buddy who knew the old ways of beating the drum and we had
a bunch of food that the women fixed. The shaman did what he
called the Brave Dance and one of my uncles looked at me and
said, 'what a bunch of crap.' I remember that 'cause it kind of
spit on my daddy, you know?

"Some of the men picked my daddy up and passed him
through the window of our house outside so's the dead wouldn't
go by the same path that the living did. Didn't want the dead
casting bad shadows.

"We buried Daddy here. Wasn't no road then. Just a trail.
They let me hammer a couple of nails in the grave house. I
think it was this one and one other," Charlie said, picking at
a rusty nail head with his fingernail. "You gotta leave open-
ings in the house so's the spirit can get out. See how there's
some shelves inside? That's where we put food for the spirit. I
expect the animals got all of it."

Charlie groaned as he straightened up. "We ain't nothin'
but old fools," he said conversationally, not to me but to the
grave house. "You and me, Daddy. What's gonna happen to
me, Daddy?"

The soft wind soughed through the tips of the pines, but
that was the only answer I heard. Charlie fished a half-pint
bottle of whiskey from his pocket, uncapped it and took a swig.

He wheezed a rheumy cough and motioned toward the road
and my truck. We got as far as the edge of the clearing and I
heard a rustling sound behind us. I turned and looked back at
the grave house. A shaft of sunlight slanted through the pines
and illuminated the center of the collapsed house. A ruffed
grouse hopped onto the ridge pole and looked across the clear-

ing at me with a bright eye. I put my hand on Charlie's arm
and he looked first at me, then saw the grouse.

The bird straightened, stretching and fluffing, then began to drum. It cupped its wings, snapped them forward, tail
braced against the ridge pole. The sound was percussive, a
muffled popping. It repeated the movement and then picked up
the tempo until the wings were a blur and the sound a muted
drumroll.

As if the impressive rataplan were not enough, the grouse
fanned its rich tan tailfeathers and erected a dark blue ruff.
It stalked along the ridge pole of the grave house, hissing and
displaying, then eased its fluffed feather and became sleek once
again.

The bird hopped off the ridge pole and scuffled through the
leaves, then was gone. I let out my breath. I looked at Charlie
and I swear there were tears in his eyes. It was tough to tell
because his eyes were bloodshot from booze and a lifetime of
squinting into weather.

It was just another summer day if you wanted to look at it
that way, with a fool grouse doing what nature programmed it
to do. If you looked at it that way.

"You want to run me on down to the house now?" Charlie
asked.

HOOKED ON FISHING

I was still a little unsettled by the experience with Charlie Pete, but it didn't stop me from continuing on to the river. I parked at a Forest Service pulloff, then hiked down a dim trail toward the river, carrying a casting rod and a small tacklebox with a half-dozen plugs in it.

The river swirled into an eddy that brooded in the sunlight before spilling over a rocky rapids and continuing downstream. Flecks of foam drifted in a wide circle and the water was impenetrably dark with tannin. It was a coffee-colored brew with the promise of big fish hidden in its depths.

I had never caught a legal musky. A couple of sub-30 inchers had nearly battled me to a standstill and I couldn't imagine the fight a 20-pounder would give me. It would be, I thought, a serious question as to who would win. Muskies show cold intelligence in their flat, alien eyes.

They look and are mean. Other fish do what they do because of genetics; muskies appear to do it because they're intelligently disagreeable.

I'd been devouring Field & Stream since I was old enough to read and someone always was tangling with a monster musky, usually in Wisconsin, often near Birch Lake. Muskies were legendary. Down at the Bluegill Bar they told stories that made muskies sound like something that would have sent St. George running and screaming.

I'd heard about the time Charlie Pete caught a musky, now mounted in the Bluegill, with a cigarette dangling from its mean mouth. It seemed like a trashy thing to do, both to Charlie Pete and to the fish, but what did I know. That's the way big guys were. Guaranteed, though, if I caught a wall-hanger musky nobody was going to stick it in a smoky bar and trash it.

It's an axiom that a 16-year-old boy with a fresh driver's license and a pickup truck is going to get in trouble. But the trouble I got in never was envisioned by any mother but mine. She was the mother of a would-be musky fisherman and having grown up in a resort town, among fishermen, she knew that where anglers go angels often fear to wade. "Nobody will know where you are," she twittered. "What if something happens to you way out on one of those rivers? We wouldn't even know where to look for you."

"Just watch for buzzards," I said. "I'll be right underneath."

"Stop it!" she exclaimed. "That's not funny!"

"He's not a baby!" my father growled. "Let him go fishing. At least he's not out somewhere getting drunk and rowdy." He glared at me. "You're not, are you?"

"No!" I protested, sounding guilty as original sin. No one sounds guiltier than when he's totally innocent protesting that innocence.

"Hmmpph!" my father snorted, rattling the Birch Lake Broadcast. He and Mr. Miller had that in common—a peevish gesture with the local newspaper that conveyed the distinct impression they thought I wouldn't amount to a hill of beans, although I'd never quite figured out how a flourishing hill of beans equated to me or any other would-be successful human.

I couldn't imagine sitting down with my father for a heart-to-heart talk about my problems, whatever they were at the moment. Or my mother, for that matter—she'd just tell me to go talk to my father. So I kept it all inside, whatever the "it" of the moment was.

We'd just finished reading Don Quixote in English Lit so, I named my pickup Rosinante, after the Don's spavined old horse. It rattled like a bucket of marbles, but it ran and got me out of the house, out of the town and into the woods and close to the water.

My casting rod was a four-foot steel Tru-Temper and the reel a Pflueger Supreme reel, handed down from my father with typical ill grace. "Well, if you're going to fish you might as well have good equipment," he said. I took the comment for what I hoped it was—a gruff attempt to hide the affection for me that motivated him to give me his fine fishing gear.

Although the rod was a light year from the willowy casting equipment just coming on the market, it still was state-of-the-art in his time. It had about the same flexibility as Don Quixote's lance and easily could have tilted a windmill or two. I figured it could whip any musky daring enough to challenge its backbone.

I tied on an eight-inch steel leader and pawed through my meager tacklebox for a lure. A four-inch Pikie Minnow sprawled in a dirty tray, rusty hooks draped over the compartment wall. One beady glass eye peered suspiciously at me. Sometimes you just know a given lure is right one. Something speaks to you.

The Pikie was a scarred old battler, with three sets of treble hooks and dents and rips where long-since-defeated members of the Esox clan had savaged it.

Snaptail Rapids frothed at the head of a long, deep stretch that lies below Lake Chippewa. There were no access roads along the river and no other anglers. I started wading downstream, the tannin-dark water swirling around my pantlegs

The rapids gave way to sleeker water, then dark pools. Snaptail's growl faded. I began fishing the impassive water. The current was slow. The river deepened and I picked my way along the shore, slipping and stumbling on glacially-rounded rocks.

I cast slightly upstream, let the current carry the Pikie

downstream as I reeled, feeling it throb against the rod, almost like a hooked fish. The casts melted one into the other and the afternoon slipped past.

A fish hit hard and the braided line burned my thumb. But it was a smallmouth bass, about two pounds...usually a trophy, but not on a musky day. I eased the fish to me and lipped it, then carefully worked the trailer treble loose.

The smallmouth darted out of sight and I took a deep breath and worked the kinks out of my shoulders. I realized I was hungry.

I sat back on a grassy bank, pawed in my daypack and found a sandwich. The dark water slipped past as sleekly as an otter. I chewed baloney and looked at the river, my mind loose and empty, like an old tow sack.

This was what I was made for—no girls to try to fathom. No coaches yelling at me.

And then a lean fish erupted from the middle of the pool in front of me, rising as high as its tail. There was no mistaking what it was—it was a muskellunge, frozen against the dark conifers on the opposite bank for a long moment. I clearly saw pale silver side, striped like a tiger. I wouldn't claim that it looked at me as it invaded my world, but that's the way it seemed.

Then it dropped, tailfirst, back into the stream—all without a sound. There was barely a ripple where it had been.

I don't think the birds actually quit singing or the river quit murmuring over its rocks, but that's the way it seemed. It was as if everything had shut its mouth when the musky was airborne. I realized I had been holding my breath for a painfully long time and exhaled noisily.

"Jeez!" I exclaimed. "Jeez!" The sandwich was dry in my mouth.

I scrambled to my feet and stumbled into the stream. I cast above where the fish had risen, then reeled slowly, watching the line. As it crossed in front of the spot, I rushed the retrieve. A ferocious hit nearly jerked the rod out of my hands.

The musky leaped clear of the water, shaking its head savagely, then fell back heavily, splashing me. I'm in the water with that devil fish! I thought and had a vision of my bare legs being ripped and torn. I stumbled back and the fish ran. The Pflueger screamed and the line spun across my thumb, searing a gouge to raw meat.

I managed to get my right hand to the reel handle so the drag would work for me and save what was left of my thumb. The fish jumped again, bulled underwater, jolting me with its savage lunges. Once I had played tug of war with Uncle Frank's burly Lab and his sharp yanks were like this...and the dog weighed nearly 100 pounds.

I was tiring, but so was the fish. It drifted reluctantly toward me and I finally saw it near the surface, large predator's eyes looking for what had stung it. Who's got who? I thought. It was huge, the biggest muskellunge I'd ever seen. The Pikie Minnow jutted from its jaw.

I had no gaff or net. I knew better than to try to lip the fish the way I would a bass. And then I made a huge mistake.

As the fish slid into the shallows at my feet, I reached down and started to slip my right hand in his gill. As if it had been waiting, the fish thrashed violently and drove a hook from the front treble completely through my already injured thumb. The pain was immediate and shocking.

"Yeowwwww!" I shouted. The fish surged toward deep water, dragging my hand with it. I dropped the rod and grabbed for the fish with my free hand. The musky wrenched sideways and neatly skewered my other thumb with a hook from the rear treble.

The barbs of both hooks were completely through the fleshy parts of my thumbs. In shock, I fell backward, sitting in the shallows. I pulled the fish toward me and clamped it between my knees, desperate to ease the weight on the hooks. Then I trapped the musky between my elbows and leaned backward, dragging it on top of me.

We were nose to nose and I realized he had one treble hook

left, the middle one. All I needed was a hook through the lip to
augment those already through my thumbs. I squirmed away
from the Pikie. The musky writhed, but I clamped it tighter
and it gradually subsided.

The rear treble had driven through the gristle of the
musky's jaw as well as my thumb. It would take a pair of pliers to twist it free. Which I didn't have. And I couldn't have
manipulated it anyway.

For the first time I realized what a hell of a fix I was in. It
was near dark, no one knew where I was, I was pinned to a
huge, heavy musky and I was God knows how far from help.
My mother's twittery apprehension now seemed prescient and I
vowed if I ever got out of this mess I'd pay more attention to my
parents. Every child who ever has been in dire circumstances
has made the same vow.

The musky seemed dead. I struggled to my feet, hugging
the fish to me as if it were Debbie Miller. There were obvious
differences. Debbie was not coated with protective slime, nor
did she look like something left over from the Mesozoic Era.

I stumbled up the bank to a dim fisherman's trail. Stinging nettle savaged my legs, but I couldn't even scratch the fiery
itch. The agony brought tears to my eyes and almost made me
forget about the hooks in my thumbs.

Almost.

Every step resulted in a tug from the fish's weight that shot
pain through my hands and up my arms. I managed to hook
my fingers in the musky's gills on either side and that helped
some. But holding its weight at arm's length was impossible.
It was just too damn heavy. I'd managed to catch a wallhanger
and instead of being on the wall, it was hanging from my
thumbs.

I struggled on, resting about every ten feet. It began to get
dark, so dark in the woods that I could tell direction only by the
sound of the water. Finally, I heard the grumble of Snaptail
Rapids and knew I was getting closer to my good old truck.

Think of the difficulties of getting your car keys out of your jeans' pocket with your thumbs fastened to a fishing plug which in turn is fastened to a huge fish.

I finally managed to work the keys out with my fingers. They fell on the ground and I lay down with the fish to find them. The absurdity of the situation hit me. I was lying in the dirt of a remote parking area, face to face with a dead muskellunge, looking for my truck keys.

It was too much and I started to laugh, then to cry. I laughed and cried for a long time until I got some control. I snuffled and found the keys. There were a thousand and one agonizing little problems before I managed to struggle into the truck with the fish and get Rosinante started. The musky lay across the dashboard, its broad head tugging at my thumbs

I clutched the wheel at the top and let in the clutch. I was in first gear and realized that's probably where I was going to stay unless I grew a third hand. Fortunately I could swing a turn without backing up. Rosinante jounced up the rough road from the rapids, my thumbs throbbing.

Northwoods highways at night are deserted. The conifers loomed over the highway and my dim lights pushed ineffectually at the dark. It's a long way between stops. Finally I saw a beer sign ahead, the inevitable beacon of the northwoods.

The Jackpine Inn parking lot was filled with pickups as battered as mine. Loggers and potato farmers were warming up for a night of conviviality and entertainment...which I shortly provided when I bumped the door open and stumbled dragging the huge muskellunge.

"Good Godalmighty!" the bartender exclaimed, dropping the glass he was wiping.

The yammer of bar rats subsided abruptly, a pool cue clattered on the floor at the rear of the bar and the only sound was the whump of an overhead fan that moved the smoky air from one part of the bar to another.

"Anybody got a pair of pliers?" I asked shakily. My voice sounded a hundred years old.

The musky weighed 51 pounds, easily the largest of the

year anywhere within 100 miles of Hayward. It took the top prize of $250 in the annual Northland Big Musky Festival.

The doctor's bill totaled $247. I bought a new Pikie Minnow with the other three bucks.

KNUCKLING UNDER TO ROMANCE

The old Soo Line rails didn't see as many trains as they once did, but still enough to keep a station agent in place. Rusty Adams had been the agent until he got drafted and subsequently lost an arm in Korea.

I suppose I could blame Rusty for part of my impressive track record of misdeeds, but it wasn't his fault that I was too apt as a pupil—better with a baseball than with the little Martin guitar he'd bequeathed to me. Because of the knuckleball that he taught me I managed to hit my coach in the throat and become a star. I'm not sure which I was more pleased by.

The Soo was as much a part of Birch Lake as the veneer mill and the lumberyard and the Bluegill Bar. The trains were as regular as the sun in their comings and goings. Trains passed through, four or five a day, heading north from the Twin Cities to Superior and back south again.

The trains passed a quarter-mile behind our house, across a pasture. If the air was still and the night quiet and I happened to be awake I'd hear a freight clattering over the sagging rail junctions, then moaning hoarsely at the town crossing. And then it would be gone and I'd hear only the sound of a whip-

poorwill and I'd swallow hard with sudden night fear as moon-
light spilled through the window.

There were occasional passenger trains. My cousin Hal and
I would stand along the tracks and wave at the passengers who
looked impassively back at us. When we grew older we began
giving them the finger, but that got no reaction either, except
once from a little girl who looked to be maybe five or six who
solemnly returned the gesture.

I put a penny on the tracks when I was nine. Just as the
train came around the bend and it was too late to dart out and
retrieve it I had a horrible prevision of the penny derailing
the locomotive which would plow into the mill woodlot, killing
everyone on board.

And it would be my fault. As the steam screamed from the
ruptured engine, mingling with the shrieks of the maimed, the
bloody engineer would stagger over to the town constable, old
Elmer Blosser, and gasp, "It was a penny. One uh them goddam kids put it there! I saw it just before I hit it! Oh God!"
and he would quiver like a shot rabbit and keel over dead.

And Elmer, whose gut was about one million times larger
than his brain, would draw his rusty old pistol and come looking for a terror benumbed nine-year-old kid.

I knew it would happen. I was having one of those frightful
experiences I'd read about in Reader's Digest ("I Saw Death's
Terrible Face") where someone has a prevision of disaster. I
shut my eyes and waited for the crash, my nerves singing. But
the train went past just as it had done for all my life, and I got
weakly to my feet and looked for the penny.

It had been jostled off the track by the train's approach and
hadn't been touched. I never tried that trick again. It was bad
enough to do the stupid things I often did unintentionally without setting out to wreck a train.

Baseball season was short, crammed into spring after it
got warm and before school let out for the summer. I was Scuz
Olsen's catcher. Catching is the most unglamorous and painful job in baseball. You're sandwiched between a batter and

an umpire, imperiled by the wild swings of inept batters and the wild fastballs of inept pitchers of whom Scuz Olsen was the epitome. Your fingers belong to anyone who can break them, but your knees belong to you…which is painfully apparent every time you struggle out of the crouch. Burly baserunners do their best to body check you into eternity or shred you with their spikes. Every fielding play is tougher than anyone else's—have you ever tried to catch a ball hit straight up.

Scuz Olsen, that unlovable loudmouth sleazeball whose weakest muscle was between his ears, was our pitcher. He was strong enough to throw the ball through a brick wall but he couldn't put a wrinkle on a ball to save his life. Accordingly he either grooved pitches for fastball hitters or threw wild pitches somewhere in the vicinity of the Pleiades. Coach K, a corpulent and crude older version of Scuz, loved his erratic pitcher.

After Scuz hit six straight batters trying to throw a curve, Coach K ordered him to stick to the hummer. He Dutch rubbed Scuz's unruly crewcut and said affectionately, "Quit tryin' to be cute and just throw the damn thing."

My problem was to convince Coach K that I had a secret weapon to win ball games. That wouldn't be easy. He considered me a tribulation in comparison with which Job's plague of boils was no more than a mild eruption of adolescent pimples.

"Coach, let me pitch batting practice," I said. "You don't want Scuz hurting his magic arm." Coach K was inclined to refuse on general principles, but he was too lazy to throw practice himself and he certainly didn't want to risk the Scuz. Nobody else could get the ball over the plate.

He chewed it over, like tough meat. "Okay," he said finally. "But no funny stuff."

"Like what, Coach?"

"How the hell do I know? You just got a history of funny stuff."

I took a couple of baseballs and strode to the mound, king of my heaped-up domain. Perhaps winning a presidential election or being named the Supreme Allied Commander is as gratifying as facing a batter from that slight promontory, but I would have to be convinced. I was born to pitch, no doubt of it. I threw a few straight pitches, a la Scuz Olsen until Coach K's interest shifted to the outfield where he fungoed fly balls.

Then I threw a knuckler to Hunk Dayland. It was a beauty that floated in like a barrage balloon then dipped sharply as if it had suddenly gotten tired. Hunk swung with everything he had, missed the ball like a foot, and the bat flew out of his hand and skittered toward second base.

"What the hell was that!" he shouted. Hal trotted over and picked up the bat and flipped it toward the plate.

Coach K whirled around when Hunk shouted and he echoed, "What the hell is going on?"

"He threw something funny, Coach," Hunk said.

"Did not!" I said. After all, there was nothing funny about a knuckleball.

"He's got somethin' on the ball—spit or somthin'."

"Lemme see that ball!" Coach K snarled and I had one of those inspirations that is so blinding at the time that the possible ramifications are obscured. All I could see was opportunity. I did not see the absolute disaster that was imminent.

Coach K was wearing a glove to field the throws coming in from the outfield and I figured if he had a glove he knew how to use it. I took a deep breath, dug my fingernails into the ball... and threw the best knuckler of my short career.

Coach K stuck a hand out for the big floating baseball and it darted up his arm and hit him smack in the Adam's apple. If I had wanted to make a dramatic statement I'd certainly done it. He staggered around like the Mummy of horror film fame, making strange sounds and I wished that I had been abducted as a baby by Gypsies to Romany where they don't throw knuckleballs that assault their coaches.

The team looked at me in shock and fear. I'd created harm on a teacher—not just any teacher, but Coach K, the Attila the Hun of the faculty.

Coach K was unable to scream outrage at the team for a

couple of days, which was a blessing, but it gave him time to refine his glower, mostly directly at me. I continued to catch and Scuz continued to pitch.

We played the Edgewater Tigers at their field in mid-August. Any athletic contest with Edgewater was a grudge match and baseball games were the worst. There usually was a substantial fight, either on the field or in the stands when the two teams got together. Once the umpire, a Birch Laker, charged into the stands and assaulted the Edgewater town constable who had shouted that the umpire had "the eyes of a mole in a manure pile.

And yeah, ya eat worms too, yah dumb bohunk!" I thought it was kind of funny, but the umpire threw off his mask, fumbled his thick glasses on so he could see and went after the constable.

That wasn't a smart move in Edgewater and the umpire spent the night in the Edgewater town jail and was replaced in the game by a local who called every Birch Lake pitch a ball and every Edgewater pitch a strike, including one that bounced in the dirt six feet in front of the plate, skipped over the catcher's shoulder and hit the ump in the crotch.

Naturally our bench cheered loudly. It's always fun to see someone who has been decked by a crotch shot clutch at his knee or ankle because he doesn't want to grab his balls in front of a crowd. Unless of course it is you who has been hit. Scuz Olsen was ejected when he went to and inquired solicitously of the umpire, "Hey, how's yer knee? Ever gonna be able to pee with it again?"

So, here we were again at Edgewater for another game. "Like goin' home for you ain't it?" Scuz said to me. "You gonna catch for both teams?" He was referring to the unfortunate incident the basketball season before when I scored for Edgewater after being unsettled by the twin cheerleaders cheering for me because they thought I was cute.

I, likewise, thought they were cute also, especially the one who had apologized. I sometimes had daydreams about us getting together, despite the social pressures against such a liaison from our respective home towns. Remember the Capulets and the Amulets or whoever they were. And the Hatfields and McCoys.

Janette (or was it Annette) was in the stands along the third base line and my heart jumped. My heart belonged to Debbie Miller, but she was away at a Girl Scout camp and Annette (or was it Janette) wasn't. I still had the occasional fantasies straight from the steaming pages of a Mickey Spillane novel.

I waddled suavely over to the stands in my catching gear and said, "Hi, remember me?"

"Sure," she said. "How could I forget?"

"Which one are you?" I asked.

"I'm Janette," she said.

"You're the one who likes me," I said.

"Well...did..." she said. "I mean I still do, but...." She didn't need to say anymore. I'd insulted her terribly at the track meet and never did figure out how to apologize. I cursed myself for being a churlish fool.

Ask her for a date! I thought. Make a silly, improvisational speech about love and infatuation (which, at that time, were synonymous). Tell her we were fated for each other...maybe to run away to far and exotic lands....

She interrupted my reverie. "This is my boyfriend, Arnie."

Arnie looked like a human storm cloud. He was about six-four with muscles on top of his muscles. He looked as happy to see me as if I'd just killed his dog.

I gulped and muttered something about how glad I was to meet him (yeah, and you, too, Mr. Hitler) and hastily retreated to the infield, stumbling over my spikes. So much for fantasy. He who hesitates is lost, I remembered and also "The moving finger, having writ, moves on." If it had writ for me, the words were, "So long, sucker." And with the middle finger, too.

"You're doing it again," Coach K growled at me in the dugout. He jerked his head toward the twin. He already had seen me with them in basketball and track and now I was consorting with the enemy, albeit an enemy as cute as enemies can get.

"We're old friends," I said.

"Yeah, right," he said. "They got you in the Edgewater Sports Hall of Fame yet?" I opened my mouth and shut it again.

The two towns had agreed to alternate home plate umpires after the fracas between the umpire and the constable and it was Edgewater's turn. The umpire was florid faced and sweating. Judging from his breath he had indulged in a heated pre-game warmup at the Edgewater Tap, the town's equivalent to the Bluegill Bar. As he draped his chin over my left shoulder to see the first pitch I nearly fainted. It was a combination of Bruenig's Lager and world class halitosis and it hung in the air like a mushroom cloud. Yet another reason to take up anything but catching.

Edgewater got out to a four-run lead and then we cut it in half with a couple of runs. For Scuz it was a pitcher's battle. He was keeping his straight arrows low enough that the batters couldn't get under them and only hit screaming line drives and hot grounders, some of which we flagged down for outs.

I even contributed by tagging a man out at the plate. He came down the line like a Soo Line locomotive. I clutched the ball to my chest like a spinster having caught a bride's bouquet and gritted my teeth. The collision sent me flying a dozen feet behind home plate, but I held on to the ball. I counted my bones, hoping none of them were in more pieces than issued and decided I was still alive. "Way to go!" Coach K shouted, clapping. I saluted him smartly and took a bow. He shook his head and quit clapping.

In the third inning I singled up the middle and took a sizable lead off first base. The pitcher lobbed a throw over to keep me honest, so leisurely that I didn't need to slide back in. The first baseman ritually slapped me with the glove and I said, "Only about an hour late."

"Get you next time, Dick Breath," he said pleasantly.

I took my lead again, rocking back and forth, looking toward Coach K. No steal sign but that surely was an oversight.
I knew I could steal on the Edgewater pitcher, a gangling farm
kid with an elaborate stretch that seemed to take forever. They
say you steal on pitchers, not catchers (which is a fiction pro-
pounded by catchers to absolve themselves of responsibility).

Coach K must not have his head in the game I thought. I'll
save him from himself. So I took off with the pitch...or what
I thought was the pitch. It turned out that the Edgewater
pitcher had the most deceptive move to first of any pitcher in
the history of baseball. It was an obvious balk, but not to the
umpire who was both from Edgewater and legally blind. He
signaled no balk and I was caught in a rundown that ended
with an ignominious tag between the shoulder blades that
nearly broke my spine.

I trudged back to the dugout, my head down, expecting
humiliation. I was not disappointed. "Boys, all together now:
what is the steal sign?" Coach K asked the question in a voice
guaranteed to catch the attention of Aleuts on the polar ice cap.

Scuz raised his hand as if he had the answer to a difficult
math problem. "Forget it, Olsen!" snarled Coach K. "I'm asking a rhetorical question."

"But coach I know the answer!" Scuz exclaimed. It was
possibly the first time in his life a teacher had asked a question that he knew the answer to. "It's when you touch your
cap brim," he said. Coach K noticed the Edgewater third base
coach leaning toward us, listening.

"Oh, great!" he snarled. "Now the whole world knows."
He glared at me. "It's all your fault." I had the feeling that if
Coach K got a dose of clap he'd somehow blame me for it.

I led off the sixth inning with us still trailing 4-2 and got
around late on a fast ball and dribbled a single between first
and second. The first baseman played off the bag and I took a
lead just beyond him. Coach K, being childish, had refused to
devise a new steal sign since Scuz had loose-lipped our old one.
"What the hell difference does it make," Coach K growled. "You

don't pay any attention to it anyway."

I glanced toward the dugout and saw Coach K slowly shaking his head from side to side. I suspected he meant "No, don't steal" but I thought perhaps he was being bothered by a pesky deer fly. It was a risk to try a second steal but I figured that the element of surprise was in my favor and besides when you're already in a manure pile a little more shit won't make much difference.

I took off on the second pitch and this time I caught the pitcher napping. But not the catcher who had been waiting the entire game to demonstrate that he had an arm like a recoilless rifle. I was out by six feet.

As I trudged once again back to the dugout I could see Coach K searching the bench in fury, looking for a substitute. But it was haying season and several players were bucking bales instead of playing baseball and we were down to nine players. I'm sure he was considering playing with eight, leaving right field wide open, just so he could have the joy of plunking my ass on the bench but he decided against it, perhaps hoping that if I continued to play lighting would come out of the blue sky and turn me to a pillar of ash. Maybe he knew how toxic the umpire's breath was and hoped I'd be asphyxiated.

Aside from a continuing low growl, like a sound from an engine with a bad bearing, he said nothing. And then Scuz stepped on his hand. It was on a dribbling ball hit by the Edgewater third baseman to Scuz's right. Scuz sprang toward it, reached down for a bare-handed grab...and stomped on his pitching hand with his left foot.

He did a somersault and came up howling. No bones were broken but he had several cleat gouges in his hand and obviously couldn't pitch. Coach K looked skyward. "Why me?" he asked. "I've tried to be good."

I cleared my throat. "Coach, how about letting me pitch the rest of he game?" He looked at me as if I were a lab specimen that had gone out of control. He raised his eyes again and repeated, "Why me?" Then he gestured feebly toward the mound and I assumed I was to take over as the Bobcat pitcher.

Hunk Dayland came in to catch. Scuz went to right field where we hoped he would languish, unbothered by fly balls. We shifted position until we had nine players more or less where they were supposed to be and I strode to the mound. What a proud moment! I was master of all I surveyed. It was a heady feeling like when I was a little kid playing King of the Hill on a dirt mound and gained the summit and defended it against the other little boys scrambling up the slopes.

My first warmup pitch was about four feet over the catcher's head. It clinked off the screen. It takes practice to learn to pitch downhill. Gradually I brought my delivery down and by the time the first batter stepped in I was in the strike zone. My first pitch was right at his head and he toppled out of the way and leaped up, shouting at me. I picked up the rosin bag and fluffed it. You don't apologize for throwing a knockdown pitch, even if it was an accident.

I glanced toward the Edgewater stand and saw Janette and her boyfriend laughing together...at me. She was making gestures and it took no expert at Pantomime Quiz to figure that she was recreating the basketball game episode for Mr. Muscle Beach.

She pumped her arms, like a cheerleader, then mimicked dribbling and watching the ball bounce into the stands. Arnie, the Man Mountain, guffawed. She made an idiot face, slackjawed and vacant. Supposed to be me, no doubt. Arnie whooped. My face flamed and I actually felt tears well. Tears of anger. I gritted my teeth and gripped the baseball as if I were trying to squeeze blood out of it.

I was fed up with being the butt of everyone's cheap shots—Coach K, Scuz Olsen, Arnie, Janette (or was it Annette)—the hell with the whole damn bunch of 'em. My next pitch was right down the pipe and it popped in Hunk Dayland's glove like a rifle shot. He wasn't much of a catcher, but he was big and tough and if he couldn't stop pitches with the glove, he'd do it with his body.

I threw another fast ball past the Edgewater batter, pretending Hunk's glove was Arnie's face. Strike two. Then I
threw the knuckler. It ambled along, looking like the moon,
and the batter nearly dislocated himself swinging at it. He
missed it a foot.

"Goddam illegal pitch!" he shouted at the umpire. "He's
throwin' a spit ball!"

"I'm throwing a knuckleball, you meathead!" I shouted
back. "And there's nothing illegal about it!"

"Lemme see that ball," ordered the umpire. Snarling, I
threw him the best knuckler ever. It did a commendable boo-
gie-woogie, darted under his outstretched hand, and boomed
off his chest protector like a bass drum. "Jesus!" he exclaimed.
"You're outa here!"

Coach K erupted from the bench, heading for home plate.
"You leave my pitcher alone!" he shouted. My pitcher! It had
a ring to it. He and the umpire stood jaw to jaw, yammering
while I wandered around the mound, kicking at dirt and feeling very satisfied with myself. I glanced to the stands and saw
Janette and Arnie with what I interpreted as glum expressions,
although they probably were simply bored.

Finally the two men finished examining each other's ances-
try and the umpire grudgingly admitted that the knuckle ball
was legal. I was still seething and proceeded to pitch a no-
hitter the rest of the way. I struck out seven of the 11 batters I
faced, six on knuckleballs. We won 8-4 and the game ended on
a piddling popup that I caught barehanded.

I wanted to throw the ball at Arnie and shout at Janette,
"Souvenir for you and your lunkhead boyfriend," but I didn't because I knew Arnie would use the ball on me as a suppository.
I juggled the ball for a moment, then dropped it on the mound
and walked toward my old pickup truck. My arm was numb,
as if I'd pulled every ligament, tendon and muscle in it, which
I probably had. I suspected I'd just left my pitching career on
that untidy heap of dirt behind me, but I didn't care.

"Nice game." It was Coach K and he was smiling at me. It

took a long moment to recognize him without his usual scowl. I checked behind me to make sure he wasn't talking to Scuz, but, no, it was me.

I nodded. Lose a girlfriend, win a coach.

That's life.

SENIOR TRIP

It occurred to me that my relationships with the opposite sex often hadn't been working out, even when I did the right thing—probably for the wrong reason, but still the right thing. It happened briefly on the senior trip to St. Paul a couple of months earlier when Debbie and I still were an item (not "Today's Laugh"). I befriended Janie Nordstrum, a girl in our class and then with typical shamefulness I betrayed her.

Debbie, a year behind me, wasn't eligible for the senior trip, so I was on my own. Janie Nordstrum was built just like one of her father's Holstein heifers, except her skin was Scandinavian fair, not black and white. She wasn't fat, just blocky and strong. And she wasn't dumb either. Just blocky and strong.

Scuz Olsen discovered just how strong one day in the hall when he offered to milk her. Scuz never met a crude remark he didn't like. He grinned his possum grin and said, "Hey, Janie, how's them milk cows? How about I milk you?"

There was a moment of shocked silence among the students who heard the remark, then Janie punched him in the stomach so hard he threw up on the gritty tile hallway floor of our old school building.

He managed to get his wind just before she vanished up the steps to the second floor and groaned, "I meant your old man's cows!" But she knew what she'd heard and she was right.

"Looks like she's fat," Scuz wheezed, rubbing his aching stomach. "Got muscles like a goddam Packer's guard."

No one sympathized with the six-foot four-inch Scuz, who had buck teeth and big eyes like a chipmunk and the complexion of a half-cooked roast. His mouth constantly ran far ahead of what passed for his brain and we all figured anything bad that happened to him was good.

On the other hand, no one wanted to date Janie. She was just too big to date. She needed to date a Packer's guard, not any kid in Birch Lake High. She had a pretty face and flaxen hair, sharp blue eyes and a bright smile.

And she had broad shoulders and stocky legs. She was intimidating. You couldn't visualize taking Janie out to the town dump for some cuddling. Especially after seeing Scuz lying on the hallway floor in a puddle of vomit.

So, boys didn't ask her for dates and with typical male crudity they made jokes about her. "Wouldn't even need a car to take her out," Scuz said (making damn sure she wasn't near enough to hear him). "Just slap a saddle on 'er and ride 'er."

A boy dating Janie would be kidded mercilessly and no boy would risk that. Secretly I thought it was a shame that anyone so pretty should be so ignored, but my sympathy didn't extend to asking her for a date, even if I hadn't been going with Debbie Miller.

The Senior Trip always was a medieval pilgrimage with all the attendant hardships. You banked on the slim odds that the end might justify the travail. We figured St. Paul had illicit pleasures we couldn't imagine in Birch Lake.

The seniors groaned in unison when it was announced that Coach K would be one of the trip chaperones. He was beefy in a coach-like way, a combination of the hard-muscled football player he had been as a kid and the suet-bound slob he was lumbering toward. He was the person for whom the term "male chauvinist" had been invented.

Coach K who earned his nickname long before the guy from

Duke and instead of a long name consisting largely of conso-
nants, our Coach K's surname was Krumhead, a name guaranteed to generate locker room puns that would gag a goat.

Coach K believed that women drained the vital fluids from
men. They were sea anchors holding back the Good Ship
Macho. According to him, the Devil had issued Everywoman a
pair of clippers at birth with instructions to give each budding
Sampson a brush cut.

If he had his way the senior trip would have been boys only
and we'd have gone to a baseball game while the girls stayed
home in Birch Lake to slop the hogs and darn our socks.

The boys weren't happy either. We figured he'd take us over
to the University of Minnesota track and make us run wind
sprints and do pushups so we'd be too tired to get in trouble.
"Boys," he said solemnly in the locker room, "Your juices are
the only things between you and being a girlie-boy. Do I make
myself clear." Not really, but no one wanted to ask him to explain.

It was a 200-mile bus trip to St. Paul. We were to stay in
a hotel, visit the Science Museum, tour the state capitol, have
a dinner at the hotel, then bus home the next morning, ex-
hausted, broke and, in common with generations of Birch Lake
graduates before us, wondering what was supposed to have
been so much fun about it. But the unknown always holds the
potential for fun, with the possible exception of death, so we
made rude jokes in the chilly early morning, waiting for the bus
driver to show up.

He was a dour Swede with the disposition of a maximum security prison guard. "Don't go spittin' on the floor," he growled
at Scuz, whom he'd once caught doing just that en route home
from a basketball game. "You spit on my floor and I'll make
you lick it up an' I'll drop your ass somewhere near Hudson."

"Don't get your bowels in an uproar," Scuz cawed. "I'm
savin' my slobber for a better bus than this old rust bucket."
And he blew a spit bubble and the driver snarled and half-rose
from his seat.

"Knock it off, Olsen!" Coach K growled. But he was secretly proud of Scuz who was the only person at Birch Lake High School as crude as he was.

Scuz fled down the aisle, giggling. As he passed me he bumped me with his hip into the vacant seat beside Janie Nordstrum. I sprawled awkwardly, nearly in her lap. She had been looking out the window, probably to avoid eye contact with boys who then would pass her by, leaving the seat conspicuously empty.

But she turned to see a boy actually sitting with her. Eyes widening, she gave me a big smile. I started to get up and the smile abruptly faded. She looked down with a fleeting, hurt expression, and turned back to the window. I paused halfway out of the seat, then settled back into it. Scuz may have put me there, but I didn't have to descend to his level by rising. "Hi, Janie," I said. 'How you doin'?" The smile returned, a nice one, and she shrugged.

"If I was home I'd be helping with the milking," she said. "This beats that. Cows are so neat, though. They're so sweet and soft and warm early in the morning. I lean up against them and feel them breathing."

"I've heard about cow tipping," I said. "You go up to a sleeping cow at night and tip it over...." I stopped, seeing the outraged expression on her face. "I've never done it," I said hastily. "I wouldn't, I mean, the only time I've been close to a cow it stepped on my foot and nearly broke it...."

I could see that my side of the conversation had the effect of Moe, Larry and Curly Bill playing with a dead chicken. "Look," I said. "Tell me about cows. I really want to know." She gave me a long look, judging I suppose whether I was serious or getting ready to do a Scuz Olsen number on her. I put on my most earnest expression.

So, we talked about cows, or rather she did. It was a revelation. Janie knew cows—she had lived with them since birth. "I get up at 5 a.m. and help daddy milk," she said. I visualized an 800-pound puppy. It sounded peaceful, leaning against the gently heaving side of a large, warm animal in the tiny hours when the rest of the world was asleep. I hadn't expected cows to be so interesting. "You can't get mad at anything when you've finished milking," she said. "Cows are so gentle and sweet that it rubs off." Probably a lot of cow sweat too, I thought, although I didn't say it out loud.

We were into cow genetics by the time the bus rattled across the St. Croix River and turned south into St. Paul. I'd rarely talked so easily with a girl before—really only Debbie. This was Janie Nordstrum who outweighed me by 40 pounds and who had left Scuz Olsen scrabbling on the floor in a puddle of his own vomit. Scuz would lose no chance to even the score with her and with me. Together we were a target as big as a Holstein milk cow.

We checked into the hotel and I thanked God that I wasn't rooming with Scuz Olsen. Hunk Dayland was built like a boxcar and was just about as much fun to talk to, but at least he wasn't fond of throwing water-filled rubbers out the window. That appeared to be the major use of rubbers as far as I could tell. Guys bought them from machines in the Rice Lake gas station (no one wanted to get caught buying one in Birch Lake) and they carried them in their billfolds until there was a tell-tale round mark on the outside of the billfold. Then they lived in terror that their mothers would notice the scarlet brand.

The trip to the Science Museum showed us far more than we ever wanted to know about the South American rain forest. I hoped there would be dioramas of naked women in the jungle, but such was not to be. I wandered off into a wing of the Mu-seum where there was a wildlife display, then realized I had to go to the bathroom. When I came back into the hall Janie was looking at a display.

"Hey," I said. It struck me that the last time I'd needed a bathroom break in proximity to a girl it hadn't worked out too well and I shuffled my feet uncertainly. There didn't seem to be any horses around. If anyone saw Janie and me together now it would appear we'd sneaked off to be with each other and I'd be inextricably linked with her. First a bus ride, then hanging out by the toilets—Scuz would have a field day.

She mumbled something, apparently aware that I was uneasy, and headed for the girls restroom. I waited for a moment, reluctant to leave, but equally reluctant to wait and run the risk of discovery. It seemed churlish to abandon her but my evil side won out and I said, "Well, see you later," into the empty hall. I walked toward the lobby, looking around for the rest of the Birch Lake seniors. There was no one I knew. The bus was not parked in front. We had been left behind.

I stood in confusion and then Janie came up beside me. "We missed the bus," I said. "We'll have to walk back." I held the door and she tried to squeeze past me. We stuck in the doorframe, grunting with effort, then finally popped through. God! It was like the Three Stooges, minus one.

My first thought was to invent some excuse to walk back by myself so I wouldn't be seen arriving with her. But there were derelict types within sight who looked as if they were waiting for a sweet-faced, blond Birch Lake Scandahoovian to molest. This was not Birch Lake—I was in a big city with no more idea how to survive than if I'd been in the Amazon rain forest with poison-darting pigmies, piranhas and hungry ocelots.

It was my duty as a he-man and protector of the fragile female to keep the slimeballs at bay. I'd just made up my mind to bite the bullet and walk Janie back to the hotel when there was a tremendous crash just behind us. A farm truck had collided with a St. Paul lamppost. Shards of glass tinkled onto the pavement in the aftermath of the shocking noise.

The truck's tailgate lay on the pavement and four Holstein cows had left the truck bed and were gathered in a confused huddle in the middle of the street, bawling.

The truck driver, a grizzled farmer, clambered out of the cab and started yelling at the cows as if the accident were their fault. "You get back in the truck, now!" Not unsurprisingly the cows ignored him and continued their colloquy. Traffic began to back up and city drivers did what they always did when confronted with a traffic problem: they blew their horns.

That didn't help the already uneasy disposition of the cows which began to mill uneasily, contemplating stampede. The farmer shouted at them, the stalled drivers blew their horns, revved their engines and shook their fists. The cows were wall-eyed with apprehension.

Janie didn't hesitate. She knew cows.

She marched into the middle of the intersection, in the middle of the cow huddle, and began issuing instructions, like a quarterback with the game on the line. The cows milled around her like big puppies, obviously delighted to find some-one who understood them.

"I might have known! I told them you were in trouble some-where! Now what?" Coach K had come up beside me and was glaring at me.

"I didn't do anything," I said. It seemed he never would forgive me for scoring a goal for the other team in a basket-ball game because I'd been distracted by the other team's cute cheerleaders or for hitting him in the throat with a knuckleball at a baseball practice.

"You missed the bus and I had to stay and find you," Coach K said. "And now look what I find. What'd you do—throw a knuckler at that farmer?"

"We were just standing here..." I mumbled, gesturing to-ward Janie, who had taken hold of the halter of a cow and was whispering in its ear. She began to lead the animal, intending to reinstall it in the truck. But the farmer, turned irrational by what the city had done to him, apparently thought that some damn city girl was trying to steal his cow. He began to shout at Janie in a mixture of English and Swedish jargon, reverting to the Old Country in a time of crisis.

He grabbed the other side of the bridle and he and Janie had a tug of war with the frightened cow in the middle. Janie couldn't see the farmer over the cow's neck and also thought someone was trying to steal the cow. Misunderstanding flow-ered in downtown St. Paul.

She launched a kick at the trousers she could see beneath the cow's neck, and the farmer took a swipe at her over the top. Both missed. "Hey! You can't do that!" Coach K shouted. "You leave her alone!" After all, he was her chaperone. In answer the farmer tried another slap at Janie who ducked. The cow danced and bawled.

Coach K sucked his gut in and marched into the fray. I shambled after him. Despite what I'd learned about cows on the way to St. Paul, I had no idea what do to in this situation. I stood like the rube I was, slouched, hands dangling, mouth slightly agape, while the situation turned from confused to chaotic. While Coach K's heart was in the right place, his musculature was not. The farmer batted Coach K out of the way as if he were a gnat. Coach stumbled back into one of the cows, which promptly bucked and kicked the grill out of a fawn-colored Cadillac.

The driver tumbled from the Caddy, shrieking apoplectic imprecations, both at the cow and at Coach K. An early victim of road rage, he took a wild swing at Coach K who promptly swung back. Both missed. The farmer continued to wrestle with Janie for possession of the first cow. The other three cows, now surrounded by cars and curious onlookers, loped this way and that, kicking and complaining hoarsely, their bags flopping.

Amid the confusion two police cars arrived, red lights flashing. I remember seeing Coach K take a swing at a uniformed person and a cow step on the foot of another. The driver of the Cadillac was screaming, "Who's gonna pay for my car?"

The farmer was screaming, "Who's gonna pay for my truck?"

A hand gathered a bunched handful of my genuine Hawaiian sport shirt from Sears and Roebuck and I was spun around on tiptoe to see the world's meanest-looking policeman holding me at arm's length like a captured alley cat.

"I haven't done anything!" I squealed.

"Get in the car, kid!" he snarled. "We'll sort it out at the station.

And they did. While I had envisioned new experiences in St. Paul, perhaps debauchery in some dim den of iniquity, lit by red lights, with lissome lovelies feeding me grapes and gropes, a ride in a police car had not entered my daydreams.

We sat on a bench in the local precinct station, a chastened bunch of tourists. The Cadillac owner and the farmer left first, under orders to exchange insurance information and work it out. Apparently a policeman with some cow experience, perhaps a loaner from Wyoming, had sorted out the bovines and gotten them back on the truck. The farmer was mollified, sort of. It was our turn in the barrel.

An officer pulled up a chair and began to question the three of us. He focused on Coach K. "You're responsible for these kids!" He frowned at the coach and Coach K flushed and glowered, but said nothing. We stammered out the story which, in retrospect, sounded so damn silly that it had to be true.

"Okay," the cop finally said. "I heard enough to know I don't wanta hear any more. Get outa here and go back to Bitch Lake or whatever it is."

We headed for the door and I heard the cop say to the desk sergeant, "I swear to God every time these hicks come to town everything goes to hell."

It was dark now and the streets were deserted. We walked two blocks before five shadowy figures leaped out of an alleyway and knocked me and Coach K to the pavement. "Don't move, asshole!" growled some unseen assailant, jerking my arm painfully backward. We were being mugged. The perfect ending to a perfect day.

Someone's knee pressed painfully into the small of my back and my lower lip was turned out by the gritty concrete and I drooled on the dirty sidewalk Coach K lay facing me, his expression that of the steer next in line at the slaughterhouse. A tough-looking kid with greasy long hair and sideburns knelt on his back, a knife blade glittering at the coach's neck.

I glimpsed Janie sideways with my top eye. The other one was blurred by tears and sidewalk grime. There were two young hoods facing her. "Hey, baby, you're built for comfort not for speed," said one and they hooted with laughter.

"Come on baby, shake your booty!" one exclaimed and he reached for her and she slapped his arm away.

"Whoa! Mama thinks she's tough," the kid said, his tone gone mean and cold. He crouched and moved toward Janie and an amazing thing happened. She absolutely cold-cocked him with a right jab that caught him flush on the nose and mouth. He went over backward and lay, sprawled, blood spurting from his crooked nose.

Before the second thug could react Janie kicked him between the legs and he doubled over with an agonized groan. "You creep!" she shouted and straightened him with an uppercut that sent him over on his back next to the other hood. Then she started toward whoever was holding me down.

"You slimeball!" she shouted. "You all think you're so tough!" I lost the rest of what she said because the weight on me shifted off and my tormentor exclaimed, "Woman's nuts!" I heard running footsteps receding. The two felled hoods groaned, rolled over and then struggled up and stumbled into the night.

I sat up. The gang was gone. Coach K rubbed at his neck and looked for blood. There was none. We were physically undamaged. Psychologically we were a train wreck. Janie stood with her back to us, stocky and with her fists clenched, breathing heavily.

"Jesus!" I whispered. I wiped sidewalk grit out of my mouth, then spit. God knows what horrible germs I'd sampled. As a protector of damsels in distress I was on a par with Don Quixote, except that he had a certain pathetic nobility. I just was pathetic.

Janie turned and we looked at each other. "I never saw anything like that," I said. "You just about killed those guys."

She burst into tears. I didn't know what to do. I patted at her shoulder awkwardly. "It's so dumb!" she exclaimed. "Just dumb, dumb, dumb!"

"Aw, you did great!" I mumbled, not knowing what to say.
She glared at me, her face wet with tears. "Gee, thanks,"
she said. "I'm just wonderful at beating the shit out of guys."
I was shocked—never heard a girl use that word before. She
wiped at her face, turned and stalked away in the direction of
the hotel.

Coach K cleared his throat, a sound like gravel falling down
a rainspout. "Maybe we oughta not say anything about any of
this," he growled. "I mean, nobody's hurt or nothin'."

Except, I was pretty sure, Janie Nordstrum was bearing
wounds that didn't show.

I looked at Coach K, who shuffled his feet and looked down
at the sidewalk where the scuff marks of his humiliation still
showed. He was acting exactly the same as his players did
when he was chewing their asses.

I didn't say anything, but started after Janie. A lone female
in the dark streets of a big city was a target, but I was pretty
sure Janie was safe. It was me I was worried about. Coach
K came along behind me, terribly embarrassed. He'd been
mugged in front of one of his players and had been rescued
by a girl, one of those manhood-draining creatures of his dark
imagination.

What would Scuz Olsen say when it turned out his hero,
Coach K, had been saved by a girl, the very same girl who had
beaten Scuz into vomitus? Coach K shuddered as the thought
passed through his mind like a piece of shrapnel.

"You know, let's just forget it," he said again from behind
me. The pleading whine in his voice was like John Wayne beg-
ging a bad guy not to muss his hair.

I wasn't about to tell anyone. Such status as I had would
not be enhanced by telling how I groveled in the dirt while a
girl rescued me. But I also was not going to tell Coach K that
he could depend on my silence. After all, weapons are where
you find them and this was a big, big club just handed to me.

Janie was a half-block ahead when we reached the hotel
and by the time we came into the bright lobby she had van-

ished. I went to the dance that night, determined to ask Janie to dance, no matter what Scuz Olsen thought about it or what he would say.

But she didn't show up. She must have stayed in her room. I convinced myself that I was coming down with a dread disease from eating sidewalk and went to the room and went to bed.

Hunk Dayland woke me before dawn and I stumbled around in a daze getting my overnight bag packed, then went to the bus. There was early morning fog in St. Paul and the bus idled with a diesel stink. I threw my bag in the cargo bay and waited in line to get on. I didn't see Janie in the near-darkness. St. Paul at dawn was nearly as depressing as St. Paul after dark, but at least no one was threatening me with a knife.

Janie was sitting halfway down the bus in the window seat and there was a girl next to her. I hesitated and Janie looked at me in the dim yellow overhead aisle light. Neither of us said anything and then she turned and looked out the window.

"Cummon, doggie, move it or lose it!" It was the bray of Scuz Olsen just behind me, and he pushed me forward, past Janie's seat. Coach K was a couple of rows back and our eyes met and each of us then averted them. "Move on, dinglebutt," Scuz said. "Slow as the seven year itch."

"Shut up Olsen!" I snarled, swinging an elbow back into his ribs. "Just shut up!" I found a seat and slumped into it, ignoring Scuz's loud threats.

"Knock it off everybody!" ordered Coach K from ahead and the bus quieted. It was a horribly long ride back to Birch Lake and we didn't talk, just dozed uneasily. I dreamed about bawling Holsteins with strings of mucus hanging out of their noses.

PROM NIGHT

The Senior Prom lurks in your future during all four years of high school, clouding the future like finals week or root canal work. It is a savage rite of passage as traumatic as ritual circumcision.

From the day you enter high school you know it's coming a runaway freight train, loaded with high explosives, gathering speed as it heads down a long, steep grade toward an inevitable cataclysm.

Our senior year began to wind down, a sloughing off like a snake shedding its old skin. The teachers were looking ahead to three months of freedom and doled out dumb make-work to keep us busy until the last day but there were no tests, no onerous assignments.

We seniors had only to fret about the prom. I had a built-in date with Debbie Miller—that was a given, considering we'd been going steady (except for the unfortunate episode with Becky Ann Garner) for years.

But somehow it was a different date, given that it would be our last formal encounter before we trotted across the Birch Lake High stage to get our diplomas, whoop and throw our mortarboards as high as possible (hoping we could get one back since they were rented).

It was special and I wanted to make it so—this wasn't a fishing trip to Thirty Three Creek or a canoe paddle to the Narrows and back. It was a formal affair.

My cousin Hal had impetigo on his upper lip and was considered as desirable a prom date as Vlad the Impaler. Prom Night can mark you for life. There are people who leap under moving buses because of things that happened to them on Prom Night decades before.

At Birch Lake High it didn't matter what you'd done for four years, what grades you'd made or how many honors you'd accumulated. You could be an American Legion Honor Scholar with a scholarship to Shoot U., but if you didn't have a high-grade date for the senior prom, one rated there by the arbiters of the student body, you had flunked high school. And no date was considered perfect by the girls who thought THEY were perfect.

Those girls among the students who were less than beautiful were categorized as "Alpo eaters" and the guys taking them to the Prom as "losers who couldn't find anybody else desperate enough to go with them." On the other hand if a girl was so beautiful as to be beyond normal criticism, she was labeled "so stuck up she thinks the world gets up when her alarm clock goes off."

I don't know how they rated the boys, but I suspect I fell into the "green as grass and twice as dumb" category. No matter—I had a date and anyone who didn't love Debbie Miller could kiss my ass.

On the other hand a certain tedium had entered our relationship. More to the point, we took it for granted that the other would be there when needed and there were times that, like a baby bird, I yearned to fly to new horizons. It is ever thus among young bucks who can't see the trees for the forest.

Debbie and I had known each other since kindergarten which had come to mean a date with her was like a date with my sister (or so I imagined—I didn't have a sister). We'd never had a formal date. We spent our time fishing or otherwise grubbing in the Birch Lake outdoors. One time after I got my decrepit pickup truck, Rosinante, we did go to the drive-in movie in Rice Lake...because it was showing "The Creature From the Black Lagoon."

All around us teenagers were ignoring the action on the screen while they swapped spit, but we watched the movie. That's why we went. Debbie was my best friend and I rarely thought of her as a girl, at least not one of the lust-dream girls.

I even briefly thought about getting another date for the Prom. Susie Anderson, the head cheerleader, was engaged to a West Point cadet and I figured that even if she did agree to go with me he'd come home armed with the technology of modern warfare and make me a bit of military history. Ellie Norgard was cute and exciting, but I dallied and she accepted a date with Hunk Dayland who looked like the side of Mt. Rushmore that didn't have presidents carved on it.

I did think of Debbie of course, but she was a year behind me in high school and I could hear Scuz Olsen braying, "Hey, guy, you robbin' the cradle again?"

It sounds dumb but I'd never thought much about Debbie as a romantic friend. She was just my buddy and I'd never been forced to the wall for a date with her—if we wanted to go to a movie we went, but it wasn't a "date" thing; it was just Debbie and I hanging out.

This wasn't going fishing; this was dinner and a dance, with a corsage, formal wear and all the trappings. This was...well, this was a date.

"Hey, how you doin'?" I ritually asked Debbie before class two weeks before the prom.

And she ritually answered, "Okay. You?"

And then for whatever reason we waited while the silence stretched on for several thousand years and civilizations rose and declined. It was downright uncomfortable. I cleared my throat several times.

"You have a cold?" she asked.

I shook my head. She looked at the floor and I did too.

Interesting floor. Had old gum stuck to it. Then we looked up at the hall clock. "I'm gonna be late for class," she said. We waited some more while I cleared my throat several more times. "I think I have some cough drops here," she said, rummaging in her jeans pocket.

"No...look...I mean, how about...I mean...you know...will you go to the prom with me?" It was blurted out with all the social aplomb of the Three Stooges poking each other in the eye.

"Sure," she said. She looked at the clock again. "Well, I gotta go." And she left for class. So what was the big deal about getting a prom date?

My father grumbled about renting a tuxedo. "I didn't wear a tuxedo to my prom," he growled. "Next thing you'll be wanting to get married and have a bunch of rug rats and we'll have to support them too."

"And after I grow old and die you won't have to support me anymore except for paying for the funeral," I said. My father looked sourly at me.

"Here's some money," he said. His grumbling was innocuous like the farting of an old dog. It was just his way. It took me 15 years to figure that out but lately we'd been exchanging insulting pleasantries and I even caught him smiling a time or two after I'd landed a verbal shot to the chops. Chip off the old blockbuster.

He gave me $50 for dinner and a corsage and promised to pay for the tux rental. I figured with that $50 and the $50 I'd saved from summer work I could show Debbie a pretty good time. A hundred bucks when my father was a teenager was enough to support a whole family for several months.

Putting on a tux for the first time is like donning a suit of armor or perhaps a woman's girdle. But I finally struggled into it somehow and clipped on the bow tie (no way would I challenge actually tying one). My mother was dewy-eyed when I appeared in the tux. "Oh, don't you look handsome!" she exclaimed and I preened because I did look pretty cool.

My father handed me the keys to the family car and about 20 minutes of advice warning against every known sin, but especially the one where you burn in hell for denting a fender. I had spent all afternoon washing and waxing the De Soto. I cleaned out my father's fishing gear which included endless rods, reels and tackleboxes. I thought I had the detritus of angling completely excised, but there always is a surprise or two in a fisherman's car.

A block from Debbie's house I glimpsed something working its way from under the passenger seat. It was a white envelope and I pulled over and retrieved it. It was full of preserved bee grubs, little yellow maggots my father used for bluegill bait. I have no idea why they were in an envelope. Probably he had planned to give them to some buddy and forgot. There were about two dozen of them, a couple mashed, the others curled resignedly in death.

Just what I needed: Debbie picking up the envelope and having a dozen maggots spill into her lap, on her formal. About as romantic as Hal's impetigo.

I was about to be late so I stuck the envelope in my tux jacket pocket, intending to pitch it in the nearest trash barrel, forgetting that Birch Lake didn't have any trash barrels. And then I forgot the envelope in the excitement of an imminent date with my tomboy friend.

Debbie's father greeted me at the door and gave me a quick inspection as if checking for signs of degeneracy. I figured I was crawling with them. He grudgingly let me in. I gave him my best ingenuous grin, looking I'm sure like Mortimer Snerd. He pursed his lips and grunted. Debbie's mother flitted around the front room, straightening things that didn't need it and twittering about her prom night.

It was as comfortable as a hanging.

Then Debbie came in and the world lit up in a way that it never had before. I had known Debbie Miller since we were six years old, but this was a Debbie I'd never seen. She shimmered like Glinda, the Good Witch of the South from the Wizard of

Oz. I expected her to tell me to tap the heels of my spit-shined shoes together, turn around three times and I'd be in Kansas or some other God-forsaken place.

Debbie's pale blue formal eddied around her like ground fog in Heaven. Her face was luminous, so familiar, yet wonderfully different, like a famous painting finally seen in the original after years of looking at badly-printed reproduction. This was not the kid of 10 years before with scuffed knees and a snotty nose.

She was elegant and I was dumbstruck, as awkward as if I were standing on a white cashmere rug wearing cowboy boots covered with reeking sheep manure.

Debbie's mother told us to have a good time and I mumbled something and stumbled after Debbie. Clem Kadiddlehopper couldn't have done it less gracefully, yup, yup, yup.

The spring evening was soft. Little kids played tag and kick-the-can, shrieking and yelling in the distance, and there was a rich perfume of something blooming. A screen door banged down the block and a dog barked. A lone car puttered around the corner and the sound diminished and vanished. A slight breeze rattled the new leaves of a birch tree in the Miller front yard.

We planned to eat at the elegant Hoover Hotel restaurant, Birch Lake's concession to tourists with money. The rambling two-story white clapboard structure had been built in the 1920s by a lumber baron as his summer home.

When the tall trees went so did the baron, but the house remained a testament to why the woods around Birch Lake were second growth.

I should have known that things were going entirely too well to last. As we paused in front of the restaurant a rasping bellow assaulted my ears like a jackhammer. "Hey, meathead! What's happenin'?"

It was Scuz Olsen and his date, Bertha Blomquist, a vacant girl with the intellect and conformation of a Holstein heifer. She was chewing gum, or perhaps a cud. As far as I knew she

was the first girl who ever had accepted a date with Scuz. All
the other girls considered a date with Scuz in the same category as virulent acne.

"You guys gonna eat here?" Scuz said. "Great! So're we.
We can eat together." Before I could invent a lie to get us out
of this awful situation, Scuz grabbed me around the neck, gave
me a Dutch rub and then gripped my arm and dragged me into
the restaurant, the two girls eddying in our wake.

The restaurant part of the hotel was named the Bois du
Nord. "What kinda stupid name is boys doo nord?" Scuz snickered. "What's that—some kinda French shit? Why don't them
stupid frogs learn to speak English?" Scuz had a great future
as a career diplomat.

The waitress seated us with a noticeable expression of
disgust and dismay at Scuz, who seemed to have rented his
tux from Charlie Chaplin's Little Tramp. Bertha was all frills
which made her look even more like a decorated heifer. Debbie didn't say anything, but the body language that passed
between us was unmistakable: Get me out of this! Much as I
wanted to I couldn't think of any excuse to flee. "My aching
jock strap!" Scuz growled. "I could eat a hunnert cheeseburgers
at the Pig and Whistle on what they get for one crummy steak
here."

Bertha munched her cud and looked placidly at the table
setting. I wondered if you knocked on her head would there
be anyone home. Or would she even feel it. Perhaps Scuz had
Dutch-rubbed her skull until it was totally numb.

I glanced at Debbie, trying to apologize with my eyes, but
she was studying her menu as if there were going to be a finals
test on it.

The waitress brought salads and each was decorated with
pansies, their tiny faces smiling up at us. I had read somewhere that French cookery often included edible flowers in
salads, so I speared one and stuck it in my mouth. Not bad—
tasted like a flower looks.

"My God!" Scuz bellowed in a voice that could have been

heard in St. Paul. "He ate the fuckin' flower!"

Bertha raised her head and mooed for the first time, "I like flowers."

The rest of the meal was no better. Scuz ate like a bird dog, great gulps and slobbers. Bertha placidly chewed her cud. I felt like screaming. What I'd wanted to be a perfect evening was. It was perfectly awful. Debbie kept her eyes down, working through her meal with grim determination.

My Steak Diane tasted more like Steak Sump Pit. It was impossible not to look up and see Scuz chewing with his mouth open. It was like watching a garbage truck processing the contents of a Dumpster. We had to get away from Scuz even if it meant stabbing him through the heart with my steak knife. Surely it would be ruled justifiable homicide.

"Hey, garsone woman!" Scuz bellowed. "You got any apple pie?" The waitress, her nostrils flared as if she were downwind of a malfunctioning sewer, said that she did. Scuz said, "Well, bring me the biggest chunk you got and don't cheat me on it either." He elbowed Bertha in the ribs and gave her a wink right out of The Three Stooges Try to Get Laid and guffawed with the sound of a landslide.

"An' stick some rat cheese on top!" Scuz called after the waitress who hunched her shoulders as if expecting a poison dart between the shoulder blades. Scuz patted his gut and I gritted my teeth against the inevitable belch. When it came it sounded like close support artillery.

Scuz interrupted his tribute to vulgarity to announce, "Hey, I gotta go drain the lizard." Debbie winched, but Bertha merely gazed upon her pasta as if it might contain the secret to intelligence. "Don't do nothin' I wouldn't do while I'm gone," Scuz added. Bertha peered after him as if wondering who he was. She must have the IQ of a chicken I thought. But she's more tolerable than he is by several light years.

The waitress brought Scuz's slab of apple pie, topped with coarse-grated cheddar cheese and set it down as if wishing it were a time bomb to which she had the trigger. I tried with my eyes to communicate that we were fellow victims of Scuzziness, but she apparently regarded me as an accomplice and hurried off.

I looked at the piece of pie with the little yellow curls of cheese on it and something niggled at my memory. They looked like something familiar and then I realized that they looked exactly like the bee grubs in the envelope in my pocket. A sudden, terrible inspiration took my breath away. It was so awful and idea that I knew instantly I would do it.

I slipped the envelope into my palm, then, pointing with my other hand, said, "Isn't that Mrs. Comstock over there?" The girls looked away and I quickly sprinkled the maggots over Scuz's pie, then crumpled the envelope and dropped it under the table.

"Wouldja believe it, they got crushed ice in the whizzer!" Scuz bellowed as he rejoined us. "Whoa, doggies! Look at that pie!" He flopped into his seat and as he picked up his fork, I said, "We have to go—Debbie has to go by her house and check with her dad about something."

She frowned at me, but I dropped money for the meals on the change tray and propelled her insistently toward the door. "Don't ask questions," I whispered. "Just keep moving."

I glanced back to see Scuz shovel a big piece of pie into his mouth and start chewing. "Hey, Scuz," I said. "That pie didn't look right to me. I'd check it out if I were you." As he looked more carefully at his plate I hustled Debbie out the door into the soft spring night.

There was a bellow and the clatter of smashing crockery behind us. Debbie started to turn, but I pushed her on toward our car. I started to laugh, a laugh that had waited for years to be born. I leaned helplessly against the car and whooped, tears running down my face. Then I hugged Debbie hard and said, "I'll explain on the way to the dance."

The town constable was huffing toward the hotel as we left. "Let's go dancing," I said to Debbie. "Life is wonderful."

Art Lundgren and the Jackpine Mellotones were playing

a Scandahoovian version of "I'm Getting Sentimental Over
You" and the gymnasium was dimly lit. Art wore a gold lame´
jacket and his hair looked as if it had been sprayed with Texaco
30-weight motor oil. The Mellotones didn't know any song
copyrighted after 1944, but mostly they refrained from playing
the polkas and schottisches that were their stock at the Breezy
Point Resort.

Debbie felt strange in my arms. This was not tackle football; it was dancing with a soft human being of the opposite
sex. I held her as if she were fragile china. She responded
smoothly to my clumsy foxtrot. I looked at her and she giggled,
thinking about Scuz trying to explain to the constable why he
had come unglued in the Bois du Nord.

Her eyes sparkled in the colored lights gyrating overhead. I
realized I had never been this close to Debbie except once years
before in a pickup football game when we all piled on and she
was on the bottom and I broke her collarbone. This was far
less painful for both of us.

I eased her closer to me as the Mellotones muddled their
way through "In the Mood." Her hair smelled of summer pastures and soft wind eddying through the pines of the Blue Hills.

"You're beautiful," I said wonderingly. "I never knew you
were." Mr. Observant, as suave as David Niven's septic tank
cleaner. She squeezed my hand, reading through my clumsy
phrasing to what I really meant.

"And you're handsome," she whispered. No one except my
mother ever had said that to me. It sounded nice.

The Mellotones knocked off at midnight and there were no
all night parties at Birch Lake High. Scuz had not shown up
at the dance and neither had Bertha. I hoped that she had
been let go as an unwitting (deliberate word choice) accomplice,
while the authorities shipped Scuz to a remote island off the
coast of Africa where he would spend many, many days swatting tsetse flies.

I held Debbie's hand as we went to the car and I thought
briefly about doing what every other couple would be doing,

parking on a secluded county road to play kissy-face. But it didn't seem right somehow. She was too perfect to smear.

She was like an artistic birthday cake, decorated with such taste and precision that you hate to cut into it. She was a Christmas package whose wrapping was pristine with promise, but so perfect in itself that you don't want to spoil the anticipation and the appreciation by disturbing it.

So I took her home. We sat in the car in front of her house. Neither of us said anything although the silence was comfortable, and then simultaneously we blurted, "I had the greatest time...."

We laughed and I said, "I don't think I ever really knew you before." She picked up my hand and kissed it.

I knew her secret. She was a princess, no matter that she had a troll for a father. She could fool the rest of the world into thinking she was Debbie Reynolds, but I knew she was Grace Kelly. "I don't want to spoil you," I said, as if she were a parfait not to be left in the sunlight. She smiled as if she knew exactly what I meant and that, too, was a measure of her princessness.

I walked her to the door, praying that Mr. Miller, he of the world class glower, would be dreaming of ripping the limbs off his daughter's suitors and not awake to do it in reality. I gave her a formal little bow, like one I'd seen Lawrence Olivier perform in a movie. "Are you all right?" she asked. "You didn't hurt your back dancing did you?"

I still wore the remnants of the silly stretched grin that Scuz Olsen had generated. I leaned forward and hugged her gently, dizzy with the soft, sweet smell of her and the airy lightness of her being.

And then, princess or no princess, I did spoil her a little.

PASS IN REVIEW

Brad Miller was the parademaster of the annual Birch Lake Pioneer Days' parade and the glowering father of my girl friend. I desperately wanted to make a good impression on him, but once when I had dinner with the Millers I was so nervous that when Mr. Miller growled a question to me, I inhaled a bit of broccoli and whooped so hard the bit of vegetable flew across the table and landed on his shirt.

"Jesus wept bitter tears," he murmured, wiping it off.

"It's all right! It's all right!" fussed Mrs. Miller, a twittery little woman. Debbie struggled to keep from laughing. I lost my appetite.

"Maybe I could help your dad with his dogs," I said to Debbie later as we sat on the porch steps. Mr. Miller raised sleek Labrador retrievers and sold the pups to the area's duck hunters. "If he'd just get to know me a little, he might like me and if he got to like me, he might quit looking at me like I barfed in his lap."

"Well...you did," Debbie said, giggling. Her pony tail jiggled and she was impossibly cute. I pouted and she said, "Aw, give me a hug." I did, nervously, afraid that Mr. Miller would see me in a chaste clinch with his daughter and rip my arms off.

"Why don't you go ask him?" Debbie said. "All he can do is

say no." And rip my arms off, I thought. I took a deep breath and went back in the house. Mr. Miller was reading the Birch Lake Broadcast, the weekly newspaper, when I made my offer. "I mean, like, I could clean out the dog pens or whatever you need done. I like dogs," I said.

He cleared his throat and smiled. It was, I think, supposed to be a friendly smile, but came across more like the bared fangs of an alpha wolf. "I don't believe so," he said, choosing his words carefully. "It's not that I don't like you. You seem reasonably bright, but I'd say you have a future about like Jake at the filling station and I'd rather not see Debbie spending her life with a Jake." He looked expectantly at me, as if seeking my agreement.

"Well, I'm not gonna work in a filling station," I said weakly.

"Maybe not," he said. He pursed his lips and added, "I can't really keep you away from Debbie, but at least I can keep you away from my dogs. Nothing personal." He gave me that wolf-ish grin again and I shuffled from foot to foot, feeling sweat pop out on my forehead.

"Well, thank you," I said. "Uh, thank you."

"It was my pleasure," he said, returning to the paper with an impatient rattle of the pages, as if he had been pestered by a mosquito. "He doesn't need any help," I told Debbie.

It probably was good that he refused because I sensed his dogs didn't like me. Every time I came near their kennel runs they barked and a couple of them snarled threateningly. I'd always gotten along with dogs, but maybe Mr. Miller had been talking to them about me.

Mr. Miller ran a small construction company and had chosen the unfortunate company title: "Miller Erections." The double entendre name was tripled by the company logo, a crane with its boom uplifted. That led to quite a bit of rowdy humor, but he was bullheaded and refused to change the name.

As Debbie's boyfriend I took my share of incoming rounds, too. "Hey, you had any erections around ol' man Miller?" bawled Scuz Olsen in front of half the student body. Until that

moment I'd never really wanted to see a human disembow-
eled by a cheetah. Scuz was the Birch Lake High School loudmouth. There was no love lost between Scuz and me. Scuz was
built like a malformed L'il Abner, with big ears and unruly hair
and long arms. He had prominent incisors, like a beaver, and a
restroom wall sense of humor. He chewed with his mouth open.

Brad Miller was just leaving the house. "Gotta get things
organized," he called back into the house. He saw me and
started, as if he'd almost stepped on a snake. His hands
clenched involuntarily.

"Hi, Mr. Miller," I said with my most friendly, innocent grin.
"How's it going?" I could almost read his mind as he considered
whether to say, "It was going well until I met you." But he har-
rumphed and took a deep breath instead.

"Parade," he said to me. "Lotta work." He looked at me as
if I were an added chore, tightened his lips, then walked by me
and headed downtown.

Mrs. Miller fussed over me like an English sparrow hopping
around looking for food. She wanted to know if I needed a glass
of orange juice. Or milk. Or something to eat. "No," I said. "I
already ate."

"How about a piece of pie?" she fussed, distraught because
she couldn't cram food down my throat.

"Really, I'm fine," I said. She did this to me every time I
visited Debbie. I thought perhaps she felt that offering food
was the only way she could connect with the boy child who was
monopolizing her daughter. Or maybe she was just as nervous
as I was, never having been the mother of a maturing teenage
daughter before.

She drove me nuts.

"Now, dear, you hold down the fort while I go help Daddy
get the parade together, okay?" She patted Debbie on the
cheek, smiled nervously at me, and left. "If I ate everything
your ma shoved at me, I'd weigh three hundred pounds," I said
and Debbie laughed.

"She just wants to make a big boy of you," she said. "Yeah,

a big fat boy." We ambled down the hall to her room and went inside. It was a typical girl's room I guess, though come to think of it, it was the only girl's room I'd ever been in.

There were several stuffed animals, a bear and a pig and improbably a chicken with a crazed look. A poster of some ice skater was on the wall, The wall was papered in a floral design which would have driven me crazy if I'd waked up to it each morning—but maybe that's a basic difference between boys and girls.

The bed had a ruffled spread with a heart-shaped throw pillow on it. Seeing the bed made me really realize for the first time that I was in a girl's bedroom, not just any old room in the house. And that we were alone in that room with all the implications that carried.

I felt distinctly uneasy, but excited too—an arousal that was all the more scary because of its improper origins. When I took a nervous breath she did too. I wiped my damp palms on my jeans. "So," I said, "What're we gonna do?" We looked at each other and the charge in the air was like that just before a close-by lightning strike. What I meant with the question and what was implied were two different things.

We were unsupervised, which was nothing new—we'd been in countless unsupervised situations for years, but never with that electrical awareness that now was in the room. Where had it come from? I took a shuddery breath. "Debbie...." Somehow we had moved closer together. Perhaps it was sideways gravity that drew us like magnets of similar polarity. We were inches from each other and I leaned even closer and our lips met.

Then we flowed together, like melting solder, and swayed toward the bed, and fell onto it. Our hands were all over each other, searching for buttons, trembling. I rolled on top of her, oblivious to anything except an overwhelming urgency.

And the phone rang, right next to the bed. Debbie screamed and tossed me off her with an extraordinary burst of strength. I went airborne and landed on my back, my wind

knocked out of me. "Uhhhhhh! Uhhhhhhh!" I groaned as Debbie, flushed and trembling, picked up the phone with one hand
and fastened buttons with the other.

She listened for a long while, then said, "Mmmmm, well,
he's at the parade and I don't know when he'll be home. Probably not all day. He probably just forgot. He's really busy."

There was a long pause while my breathing returned and I
lay there thinking of worlds lost. "Well, I guess we could drive
over and get her, my boyfriend and me." She chewed at her lip,
said a few more monosyllabic things and hung up. "Daddy's really going to be mad," she said, frowning.

Fear froze me. Daddy! The dread bulldog! She was going
to tell him that I had molested her and he would use his construction implements to deconstruct me. I was speechless with
panic.

"Oh, God, don't tell him!" I exclaimed. "I'm sorry!"

"About what?" she said. "Tell who?"

"Your dad. About us doing, you know." She looked at me as
if discovering for the first time that I had no brain. "I wasn't
going to tell him," she said. The terror began to ebb.

"And why are you sorry?" she asked, a hint of anger in her
voice..

"I'm not!" I protested quickly. "I mean I am if you want me
to be," I added weakly. "Your dad scares the hell out of me."

"Well," she said. "He's my daddy." Whatever that meant.

Her lightly-freckled brow was furrowed with indecision.
"Some guy at Rice Lake has a female Lab that he's supposed to
breed with Daddy's dog. He says his vet says the dog has to be
bred today or it won't work and his car's broken down."

I was confused. "Whose car—the guy or the vet or the dog?"

She looked at me somewhat the way her father always did.
"The guy, you idiot. He wanted daddy to come get the dog, but
Daddy's so darn busy today with the parade that he can't do it,
so I told him we could come get the dog."

This talk of breeding, especially after what had been hap-
pening just before the phone rang, made me nervous again. If

there was one thing on earth I did not want to do, it was stand around and watch two dogs mate with Debbie at my side. I must have looked dubious because Debbie said somewhat tightly, "Well, if you've got another date...."

"Oh, no!" I exclaimed hastily. "No problem. Let's do it."

"You didn't bring your truck did you?" Debbie asked and I told her I'd walked over. "Well, I guess we can use Daddy's pickup. He won't mind." She found the keys and had a thought. "I don't know if we're supposed to take Ranger to, you know, kind of get introduced or not."

"Who's Ranger?" I asked.

"Our male Lab," she said. "I never paid much attention to how it works with dogs. I mean do they have to, you know, date for a while before they, well, you know?"

I almost said that if dogs were like Debbie and me, date or no date, there'd never be another puppy, but decided to keep my mouth shut. Things between us had grown uncomfortably edgy. Debbie argued with herself about whether to take Ranger and finally said, "Well, I guess we'd better. It can't hurt anything."

We went out to the dog pen. Ranger was banging off the chain link kennel fence as if it were a blocking dummy and he were an NFL middle guard. He was a beefy Labrador the approximate size of Ecuador. The other dogs yowled and barked.

I flipped the latch on the gate and Ranger bulled through it so fast that the gate slammed into me, knocking me over a coil of garden hose. I fell on my back in a slime of mud left by the leaking hose. Then the rotten dog danced all over me, including my crotch, until Debbie shouted, "Ranger, stop it! You two quit playing. We're in a hurry!" I writhed in the mud, my testicles throbbing, wishing I could whack that dog into next week with a splitting maul.

By the time I hobbled to the truck, Ranger had clambered in the cab next to Debbie, slobbering and supercharged as if he knew he were heading out on a date with erotic implications.

There was just about enough room for a Munchkin on the

passenger side and I shoehorned my way in and slammed the door. The door handle dug painfully into my hip, but Ranger wouldn't move when I pushed at him. I sighed and tried to ignore the pain. Ranger continued to crush me against the door and every time I looked at Debbie it was through Ranger's mouth, a haze of drool and white teeth and a pulsing pink tongue.

I sulked, scrunched against the door, and when Debbie said, "We'll be back in plenty of time for the parade," I didn't answer, only sighed heavily.

"Well, what's the matter with you?" she said.

"Nothing, just nothing," I grumbled. "Only your damn dog stomped my nuts and I don't have enough room to sit." She didn't answer, just drove a little faster, her knuckles white on the steering wheel.

"You didn't have to come," she said to the windshield. A few more seconds, then, "I wish you hadn't if you're going to be like this."

"Be like what?" I said, my voice rising. "I haven't done a damn thing except get stomped and pushed around." Ranger shut his mouth and a low rumble came from his barrel chest. I glared through the streaked side window at the trees flashing past.

We finished the trip in absolute silence. The owner of the female was dubious. "I don't want nothin' happenin' to Lady," he said. "I mean except what's supposed to happen. You reckon one of you could ride back there with them dogs and make sure they don't jump out or run off or somethin'?"

"He'll do it," Debbie said, nodding at me as if I were their yard boy. I thought about refusing, but it was a long walk back to Birch Lake and I'd already irritated Debbie enough. She had Ranger on her side and the keys to the truck.

The two dogs bounded happily from one side of the truck bed to the other. I started to climb over the tailgate and Ranger immediately snarled at me, his shoulder fur rising ominously.

"Oh, oh, that ain't gonna work," the man said. "That dog don't like you." Debbie looked at me as if I'd let her down. It was a look I'd seen many times on her father's face, but rarely on hers. It occurred to me that we'd crossed a border back in her bedroom and something fundamental had changed in our relationship but not for the better.

Debbie pitched me the keys. "I'll ride with them," she said. "You drive. Without hesitation, she clambered over the tailgate and the two dogs fussed happily around her, tails slinging. I climbed into the cab, sulking. Probably wreck Brad Miller's truck on the way home, the way things were going.

I peered in the rearview mirror and saw Debbie's curly blond head, framed by two square black heads. The two big dogs leaned against her with boundless affection and she knuckled their ears. I sighed and wondered why we seemed so peckish with each other. The day had started with such sunny optimism.

The hot summer wind eddied through the truck cab as I crossed The Narrows between Birch and Balsam Lake, started up the long hill toward town. Maybe I could make it up to Debbie later on, make things better between us.

I turned the corner at Jake's Sinclair onto Main Street and immediately had to stop to avoid banging into a vehicle just ahead. I peered up through the dirty windshield and saw a young girl in a formal looking down at me, a puzzled expression on her face. She wore a sash reading, I realized with mounting confusion, "Bluegill Queen."

What the hell....

And then I realized what was going on. It wasn't just any vehicle; it was the float carrying the Pioneer Days' fair queen and her attendants and it was part of the parade. I was not in ordinary traffic; I was in the parade. My God!

I threw the truck into reverse, intending to back into Jake's Station and wait, but a horn blared behind me and I gawked at the rearview mirror and saw a large implement dealer's truck on my bumper, the driver impatiently motioning me forward.

The queen's float moved ahead and reflexively I shifted to first and let in the clutch. I looked in the mirror again and this time focused on my own vehicle. Just past Debbie's shoulder the two dogs no longer were sitting placidly with Debbie. They were in the rear of the pickup bed and they had succumbed to lust.

Ranger was atop Lady, hunched over like a pool player going for a table run. Lady braced herself with resignation as if the reality of mating was far less exciting than the anticipation. The truck rocked as Ranger joyously copulated while Debbie, her hand at her mouth, shrank against the cab wall. I was frozen to the wheel, mindlessly following the vehicle ahead.

The street was lined on both sides by Pioneer Days' fair visitors, all beginning to grin and point. I had no alternative. The side streets were barricaded and there was no place to hide. Little boys stood with their mouths open, not quite sure what they were seeing. Rowdy drunks slapped their thighs and each other's shoulders. Elderly women covered their eyes in offended dignity.

Almost no one had to wonder who belonged to this unique float. They all knew Brad Miller—his company logo was on the truck—and they all knew me and Debbie. I was driving slowly down the middle of Birch Lake's Main Street with the daughter of the parademaster trapped in a pickup bed with two ecstatic dogs happily engaged in explicit, lascivious conduct. This was the stuff of town legend.

Occasionally from the blur of faces one would emerge that I recognized. Brad Miller appeared at curbside, shaking his fist and shouting something incoherent. I caught the phrases "my daughter" and "never in a million years" but the rest mercifully was swallowed by the swelling tide of laughter.

Must have been terrifically funny to a spectator: humping dogs in a truck with the logo "Miller Erections." And Brad Miller's daughter in the back watching them go at it.

Of course Scuz Olsen was on the scene, a natural phenomenon at a disaster, like fire following a lightning strike. "Hell of a float!" he shouted. "Ho, doggies!" He enjoyed it with keen appreciation, a connoisseur of other's humiliation.

Coach K, our basketball and baseball mentor, also was in the crowd, shaking his head slowly from side to side, like a sick horse beleaguered by flies. His eyes met mine and then he resumed his melancholy denial. He had been wary of me ever since I threw a knuckleball that dipped at the last moment and hit him in the throat in front of the entire Bobcat baseball team.

My mother's face was shocked and white. I shrugged to indicate my helplessness, but it probably looked like indifference. My grandmother was graven in stone, a visage from Mt. Rushmore, only more imposing.

I risked a glance in the rearview mirror and Debbie's face was pressed against the back window and she was saying words that I couldn't make out. "Your fault!" did come through clearly. I shrugged to indicate there was nothing I could do, but it must have appeared that I didn't care. She looked to each side of the street, hearing only raucous laughter and seeing pointing fingers, and she buried her face in her hands.

The enormity of the situation and my embarrassment began to overwhelm me. I felt a hysterical laugh building, swelling toward an explosion. I could not suppress it. It roared out of my mouth and it wouldn't quit. I laughed and cried and pounded at the steering wheel, tears streaming down my face.

Debbie heard me.

I felt more than heard her banging on the window and I twisted in the seat to see anger and humiliation in her face. She was shaking her fist, just like her father. She did not look like the human rainbow who had captured my heart at the Junior-Senior Prom—more like the summer storm that approaches, green and ominous.

The dogs were tied, waiting in that patient way dogs have, for nature to separate them. Ranger was panting and looked enormously satisfied with himself. Lady merely looked resigned to the universal fate of bitches.

We traveled the length of Main Street before the parade turned east and I was able to get free of it and pull into a deserted driveway. I stopped and opened the truck door, my entire body weak and drained.

Debbie already was on the ground waiting for me. She reached up and grabbed me by the front of my shirt and jerked me out of the cab. My momentum carried me forward, falling and stumbling, facefirst into a massive multiflora rose bush which grabbed at me with a thousand claws.

I sprawled there in pain, unable to move, shocked by the bite of the briars. Debbie never looked back. She vaulted into the pickup, slammed the door and backed out of the driveway, tires squalling. The sound of the truck's engine diminished and was gone. Briar by briar I picked myself free. I was covered with scratches, my new T-shirt dirty and torn, sprinkled with black dog hairs. All of Birch Lake was a block away and I was more alone than I'd ever been.

I knew our romance was over. If I just hadn't laughed. But I did laugh and she saw me do it. All of my dreams went up into the hot summer sun and I was alone with my despair.

The family was silent at dinner and I picked at my food without appetite. My father seemed to be off in the world he'd chosen for himself when unpleasant circumstances arose. My Uncle Al occasionally would begin to chortle and then choke it back at a glare from my grandmother. My mother, like Mrs. Miller, tried to salve the situation by showering me with food offerings.

I still hadn't gone to sleep when my bedside clock showed midnight.

Perhaps I could do as countless swains had done and serenade Debbie into forgiveness. I picked up my guitar in the dark silence and slipped out of the house and skulked through the town to the Miller house.

I didn't know many love songs, but did know a popular song that we considered our own—the Four Lads' "Moments to Remember." It didn't occur to me that I had given Debbie a moment she'd desperately not want to remember, but I took the guitar from its case and began to sing, softly and with aching emotion.

"Get him, Ranger!" I heard from the back of the house and there was a fearsome growl and the scrabbling of claws. With a squawk and a clang of strings, I leaped into the low branches of an old maple and desperately tried to outclimb the apogee of an enraged, leaping Labrador. Ranger snarled in frustration at the base of the tree and a light came on in Debbie's bedroom window.

She threw it open, no more than 20 feet from me, and she was backlit in a shorty nightgown. Even in my panic it was enough to make my mouth go dry. There I was at eye level with her window, the quintessential Peeping Tom. "You pervert!" she cried. "I never want to see you again!"

Ranger snarled his agreement and Mr. Miller gritted, "Get out of my tree and out of my sight!"

"I'm afraid of the dog!" I quavered.

There was a long silence while we all considered our options. Mine were limited. "Come on, Ranger," Mr. Miller said. "You can have him next time." He raised his voice to me, "I'll count to 100 and then I'm turning the dog loose." He began to count, leading the dog away.

"Count faster, daddy!" Debbie called. She was not on my side. Mr. Miller was at 50 when I slid out of the tree and desperately threw the guitar in its case. I cleared the gate at 90 and was out of sight by the time Ranger slid to a stop at the sidewalk, growling in frustration.

The Pioneer Days' fair float committee debated long about whom to award the Best Float trophy to—I was the odds-on favorite, but commonsense prevailed and they gave it to the Bobcat cheerleaders for an enormous bluegill.

Good thing. I had a prevision of where Mr. Miller would have stuck the trophy.

ROSE MARIE

Billy Boy Dam was halfway to the Brule, an old logging dam on the Couderay River. It had been named for an Ojibway chief and was within the reservation. Big muskies liked to cruise in the eddy pool below the dam because food fish stacked up there and were easy to pick off. I had brought my casting rod and figured to throw a bucktail into the wash below the dam a few times before heading on to the Brule.

The morning was bright-sunny and the eddying scuts of foam in the spill of the dam were almost hypnotic as they swirled slowly, pulsing and bobbing with the many cross currents. A raven coughed hoarsely and an osprey cruised the river, looking for food.

If I could spend the rest of my life at this spot, in sunlight, mindlessly casting, retrieving, casting again, I would be happy. I can't say I felt a whole lot better about all that had happened in Birch Lake: the disintegration of my friend Jake, my break-up with Debbie and the as-yet-unfaced humiliation from meeting townspeople one by one, but it was easier to forget about it here on the river flipping a bucktailed spinner into the bright sunlight, watching it arc through the mist of the dam rapids.

An old shack across the river leaned tiredly, as if canted

into a perpetual wind. I'd seen it before, but never paid much attention to it. There always were a couple of Indian kids fooling around in the yard, which was littered with rusty pieces of cars, broken toys and disabled furniture. The house was a crazy quilt of tarpaper and haphazard boards nailed to hold the paper in place. The metal roof was rusted and the broken windows were patched with cardboard. It had to be brutally cold in winter, unbearably hot in the summer.

As usual, a couple of Indian kids were wrestling in the yard. And then Rose Marie came out of the house and it was like seeing a flower blooming in the desert. She was barefoot and in old cutoffs, with a tube top that emphasized a full figure that was as difficult not to stare at as it is impossible not to think of elephants once someone tells you not to think of elephants.

The two little kids started scuffling, shrill voices raised in recrimination, and she scooped one up kicking and snot-nosed, and dumped him behind her, fending off the other one, keeping them separated. "Shut up or I'll throw you in the river," she commanded. They quieted instantly. I figured that more than once she'd carried out that threat, so they knew she wasn't fooling.

Rose Marie skirted the rusty geared wheel that operated the floodgates and walked across the dam, carefully avoiding the rotted places in the old planking. I cast the bucktail into the wash, letting the white water carry it downstream as I retrieved it slowly across the current. I saw her out of the corner of my eye, but deliberately did not look at her.

My experience with Indians was seeing old drunken Charlie Pete reeling down the sidewalk in Birch Lake, banging off lamp posts and muttering to himself.

"You're kinda good-looking," she said just behind me and I jumped. "Big ears and too skinny, but you got some muscle on you." I looked at her for the first time and realized she was absolutely beautiful, maybe about my age.

She grinned at me, enjoying my confusion. "You too," I said inanely. "I mean your ears aren't big and you sure aren't too skinny...." I took a deep breath and blew out explosively. "God, what a dumb butt I am!"

"How's the fishing?" she asked.

"It's okay. I mean I guess it's not okay. I haven't caught anything." I stopped just short of scuffing my shoe in the dirt, feeling like the biggest hick in the world. God! I thought, if I get any more stupid they'll send me to a Home for the Terminally Dumb.

She lithely hoisted herself onto Rosinante's shabby fender. Lucky truck. She was darkly lovely, olive-skinned, jet black hair, large brown eyes and full dark-rose lips. I figured she might be about my chronological age, but was about one thousand years my emotional senior.

One of the little kids at her house began to bawl. "Shut the hell up!" bellowed someone inside, the voice carrying clearly across the throaty gargle of the water spilling over the dam. The child subsided, whimpering. Rose Marie hunched her shoulders as if the day had suddenly turned cold.

"I'm Rose Marie," she said. I told her my name and said that Rose Marie was a beautiful name. "I named myself," she said. "When I got old enough. My mama named me Bernice and I thought that was the stupidest, ugliest name I ever heard, so I told her I wanted to be called Rose Marie."

"What did she say?"

"She said she didn't give a shit one way or another," Rose Marie said, the vulgarity as shocking as if a flower had opened to reveal a garden slug inside.

"Where you going with the canoe?" she asked.

"Up to the Brule," I said. "Do some fishing."

"Can I go?" she asked. It took a moment for the question to sink in. I gulped.

"What?" Things like this happened in daydreams, but not in my life. "Er, I'm, I mean, I'm gonna be gone overnight." Did that sound like a lewd invitation? Probably did.

So she'd snarl, "Well, if you think I'm gonna spend the night with a geek like you, fella, you're badly mistaken." Then she'd swat me in the chops and stalk off.

She smiled. "So," she said. "Who cares?"

"I...don't...know," I croaked in a hollow voice that sounded like a raven trapped in a 55-gallon barrel. "Don't you gotta ask?" I usually was careful with my language, but I sounded like Scuz Olsen at his grammatical worst.

She snorted. "They wouldn't care if I never came back, much less whether I went in the first place."

Before I could say anything more, she said, "Here, let me carry something," and she took my tacklebox. Our hands touched and the only thing I'd ever felt as soft was the paw of a pet raccoon that gently patted my face.

She put the tacklebox in the truck bed, jerked open the passenger side door and jumped in. Short of abandoning my truck and running like hell, I didn't have much choice. There was a panicky moment when I did consider running. I was way out of my depth.

I got into the truck the way a condemned man gets into the tumbrel. My God! I thought. Suppose her mother thinks I'm kidnapping her and...what? Sends a couple of crazed Indian warriors after us! Calls the highway patrol! Starts plinking at Rosinante with a .30-.30!

I jabbed at the ignition as if I were trying to gig a frog, my mouth dry, my heart hammering. I was desperately aware of her slim, lovely legs and that jutting tube top. "Well, come on," she said. "Let's go."

I cleared my clogged throat and mumbled, "Yeah, sure." I turned to her so close that I could catch a scent of pine coming from her. Probably bath soap, but it seemed like the essence of the northern woods themselves and she like a wild spirit of those dense forests. "Are you sure you want to...I mean...you know...go?"

She reached over, grabbed my T-shirt, pulled me toward her and gave me a kiss that made steam come out of my ears. "Let's go," she said.

Nothing like this ever had happened with Debbie. Nothing

like this ever had even occurred to me with Debbie, except for that fleeting, awkward moment in her bedroom. Rose Marie was no Debbie.

"Where you from?" she asked. She hiked her knee up on the seat, half-facing me and it was like being near a cherry-red stove. She radiated heat and sex and I was numbed by it, every sense on overload.

"Birch Lake," I said. "Down south of here, you know, Birch Lake."

"I don't ever go down that way," she said.

"Where do you go?" I asked.

"Hayward." She shrugged. "Dance, do a few brews, party, you know."

I didn't, but didn't say so.

"Why did you ask to come along with me?" I said. I felt like my ears were too big and my hair unruly and I was too skinny for a girl as beautiful as Rose Marie, even though she said I had some muscle on me.

"You got a cute butt," she said, shocking me again. She was light years from Debbie Miller. She was dark; Debbie bright and blond. She radiated a sexual aura you could almost see; Debbie was so sweet as to have no aura at all. But the major difference was that she was in the truck with me and Debbie was not.

We reached the river put-in about noon and unloaded the canoe. "How do we get back to the truck?" she asked.

"I figured I'd hitchhike from the campground. Sometimes people stop."

"They always do for me," she said.

She bent over to put my rod case in the canoe and my mouth went dry. There were a couple of holes in the seat of her cutoffs large enough to show that what was within was Rose Marie and nothing else.

"Where do I sit?" she asked.

"In front. You can paddle if you want to, but you don't have to. I'll take care of steering if you just want to loaf."

I admired the silky gloss of her black hair, the rich copper of her shoulders. I took a deep breath and pushed us into the current.

The Brule flowed silent and dark with tannin for the first few miles, narrow and twisting through peat marshes. The water curled and pulsed, the only sign that there was motion below the impenetrable surface.

An occasional rounded granite rock poked through, but there were no rapids. The river was sweet and the sun beat down increasingly hot. I stripped off my T-shirt and tied it around the thwart in front of me.

"You got a girl friend?" she asked.

"Did have," I said. "Till yesterday."

"You broke up?"

"You could say that," I said. "Her dad sicced his dog on me."

"Wow, what'd you do—get in her jeans or something?"

"Not hardly," I said. I started to tell her about the parade, painfully at first, then as it became cathartic and the more I talked the easier it came and when I finished, she started laughing so hard that the canoe rocked dangerously.

"God, I'da given a million dollars to see that!" And she started laughing again, a whooping belly laugh that was infectious. Pretty soon I started to laugh too and the more I did the funnier it became until I realized that I really didn't care what people thought about it.

In fact, I thought, I'd rather be me who got in an embarrassing but funny situation than Jake who lost a cat and spent six months in jail. Kind of put things in perspective.

After that things were easier between us. I told her about the time I learned to throw a knuckleball and threw one that dipped at the last instant and hit an umpire in the crotch. "You should have seen him lying there grabbing at his knee when everybody in the ball park knew the ball hit him in the nuts," I said.

I'd never talked like that to Debbie. She just didn't seem the type to tolerate crude talk, but Rose Marie not only seemed the type, she used crude language herself.

"You're cool, you know that?" she said.

"Regular ice cube," I said, enormously pleased with myself. We drifted past big pines standing dark sentinel duty on high banks. Alders swept low over the water in the swales, but I wasn't tempted to fish. Tempted, but not by fishing. Tempted by the olive beauty in the front seat of my canoe.

We bounced through the first low rapids and I deliberately steered into the one standing wave and scooped a cupful of icy water over the bow. She squealed and grabbed the gunwales.

"No sweat!" I called. "You're in the hands of a master!" She giggled, a sound like wrens in the garden.

We drifted through a long pool and I let the canoe follow the current and cast an Adams dry to several eddy pools, finally hooking a small rainbow trout, which astonished her. "I never saw no one fish like that before," she said. "My uncle uses nets and traps."

"But that's illegal!" I exclaimed and then thought maybe it wasn't for Indians. "I mean, I think it's probably okay if you're, you know, an Indian...." I stopped, embarrassed, and she turned and looked at me over her shoulder, without expression.

"I don't know what to say," I confessed miserably. "I mean, I get all screwed up around girls anyway. And you're the most beautiful girl I've ever seen and I'm sorry for being so damn dumb."

The canoe, forgotten, bumped into the bank and we both clutched at the gunwales as it rocked, then we looked at each other again, and there was something between us that transcended embarrassment and racial tension. It was like an electrical arc, blinding and powerful.

"You want to eat some lunch?" I said, my voice gone gravelly. She nodded.

We climbed to the mossy bank, amid the pines, and unpacked the food I'd brought. There were sandwiches and a couple of cans of Coke and a can of string potatoes. The eddy pool at the foot of the bank swirled slowly in the summer sun, occasional bubbles marking the dark, patient movement of the river. We were in cool shadow.

She flipped a pebble into the pool and rolled over on her stomach, propped herself on her elbows. "I never was in a canoe before," she said. "Sounds goofy, an Indian who doesn't know nothing about canoes. Let's go for a swim. I'm hot."

It took a moment for the last part to sink in. "Swim?" I said, in a voice gone high and skittery. "We don't have any suits." She smiled, as one would at a child trying to fit blocks into the right holes of a pegboard toy.

"Oh, geez!" I whispered. My throat was full of fur balls. "We just ate. Suppose we get a cramp...." I croaked.

"Come on," she said softly.

She knelt, facing me. I was rigid and scarcely breathing. Slowly she hooked her thumbs under the tube top at the sides, never taking her smoky eyes from mine. She lifted outward and up, freeing her breasts. She lifted the material up and over her head. I took a shuddery breath.

She stood up, her shadow covering my face. Her black hair fell in a soft spray over her breasts. Then she unbuttoned her shorts, drew in her stomach and pushed them downward. They slid to her ankles with a slight whispery sound. She stood before me for a long moment, alight with her sensuality, letting me see her. Then she turned quickly and plunged into the river.

"Come on, chicken!" she shouted. She splashed cold water up over the bank onto me and I yelled in surprise and scrambled to my feet. I kicked out of my blue jeans, clawed my T-shirt over my head, and dove recklessly into the pool. My nose scraped along the sandy bottom.

I came up rubbing it, to find her gone. I looked around, panicked for a moment. Then she grabbed my ankles and flipped me under water. I came up choking and spewing. She laughed and dove away from me. We sported in the water like young otters, splashing, diving, twisting and lunging.

Finally we paddled quietly to the shallows and looked wordlessly at each other. We climbed out and she came into my arms, naked and cold.

I kissed her, smoothing her wet hair back from her face. Her body warmed against mine and I ran my hands lightly and wonderingly down the soft curve of her back and buttocks.

It all seemed so natural as we settled to the springy moss on the bank. There were eagles on the wind and lovely fish just below the surface and the world pulsed like a great heartbeat and the clocks ran backward. When we finished I whispered, "I love you. I love you so much."

I never wanted to be anyplace other than in her arms on this sunny riverbank, but she freed herself abruptly and sat with her back to me, facing the river, and there was the stiffness of anger in her pose. What had I done wrong? I touched her back shyly and said again, "I love you."

"Oh, come on!" she exclaimed. "You don't love me. You love what we did."

"No, I love you!"

"You're such a kid," she said, almost sadly. "Such a kid."

I started to protest and she covered my mouth with her hand. "Don't say nothing about love," she said. "It was great. It was really great. You're not like...well, you're just nice and that's enough.

"I don't understand," I said. "What's the matter?"

"Look," she said in the tone of a weary adult explaining something perfectly obvious to an uncomprehending child, "you're the nicest kid I ever met. You don't want to be hanging around with me."

"But I do!"

"It was your first time, wasn't it?"

I hesitated, considering whether to lie to make myself seem more worldly, then nodded.

She smiled and brushed some sand off my shoulder. "Well, it wasn't for me. Not by a long way."

"I don't care!" I exclaimed, reaching for her. She scooted back, got to her feet and grabbed her shorts.

"Forget it," she said. I suddenly felt very naked. I started to pull on my shorts, got one leg caught and hopped around on one foot off balance, then fell in a tangle. It was a clownish collapse and she should have laughed.

She didn't.

"I'm knocked up," she said and my lips went numb. My God, we just did it. How could she know she was pregnant. I was going to be a father and I didn't even have a job or any money or any future.

I couldn't breath, could only wheeze.

"Not you," she said as she recognized my stricken fear. "Some guy from Hayward. I don't even know for sure who. I shot blanks the last three months you know. That's one reason I let you, cause it don't matter."

"It does too!" I shouted. "I'll marry you!" I finally got both legs through the shorts and pulled them up, trapping leaves and twigs inside. She was fully dressed now and looked sadly at me.

"Grow up," she said. "Look, we had a good time. Go find some little honey and marry her. Go back to your Dotty."

"Debbie," I corrected automatically.

"Okay, Debbie, whatever," she said. "You and me? Not in one million years."

I wanted to take us back to eagles and fish and time suspended. She looked rumpled and older, her vibrancy gone. "I'm gonna go home," she said. "It really was fun and I really like you, but I'm gonna leave."

"You can't leave! We're in the middle of the woods. How would you get home?"

"Take care," she said and she vanished into the woods, away from the river. My mouth dropped open and I grabbed for my sneakers and shouted, "Wait, don't leave!" By the time I got them on and ran into the woods after her there was no sign, no sound.

I ran for a long while in the direction she'd gone, but finally realized I could not catch her and I accepted that she didn't want me to catch her, that we were through. She'd find the highway and, like she'd said, she would get a quick ride to somewhere, maybe even home.

Rose Marie was gone from my life as abruptly as she'd entered it and I knew with sure instinct that I would never see her again. I would not go to Billy Boy Dam and try to find her. I would cling to something as evanescent as a fever dream.

That first time had been like your breath on a cold day, clear and present and then vanished. It was over so quickly and I hadn't had a real thought through the whole episode. There was the terrifying but glorious sight of Rose Marie nude and then my body took over from my mind and there was nothing but brief but overwhelming sensation, then the stunned realization that I was something different than I had been in the morning.

I wanted to go back and approach that moment with deliberation, savor every instant and make it last. I'd been like one of Mr. Miller's damn Labradors confronted with a filet mignon. Two gulps and it was gone, no stretching out the moment. I felt stupid and deprived.

Great lover I was—the dogs in the back of the pickup had more fun than I did or at least they made it last longer. I slowed to a walk, then sat on a log and felt the way migrating butterflies must feel when they're caught in a strong wind.

I realized that I had no idea where the river was, that I was lost. Downhill seemed a logical direction for the river, but for all I knew I was heading into a swamp or another river drainage. Still, there was the old Indian trail. Since an Indian had gotten me into this fix, I might as well follow an Indian direction to get out of it.

I walked for what seemed like a couple of miles and still heard no sound of running water, nothing but the occasional bird and what could have been the grunting of hungry bears, but more likely was two trees rubbing together in the wind.

Panic grows, like a noxious weed. At first I was concerned, but I knew the woods (not these woods, unfortunately, but woods in general). I could figure out where I was and if I kept to a line I'd hit a road sooner or later. Of course later might mean dark. Suppose I did come to a road. Which way would I turn? I squinted through the trees and, sure enough, the sun was getting low. It was late afternoon, but I didn't know how late. The only advantage of living in a northern state in the summer was that the sun stayed up almost until bedtime.

But I didn't want my bedtime to mean sleeping against a tree, no light source, no matches, nothing but indefinable night sounds. Sure, I knew intellectually that I was the most dangerous animal likely to be in the woods after dark, but my fears began to overwhelm my good sense.

I started trotting, then broke into a run, jumping glacial rocks and root wads, my breath beginning to rasp. I knew it was stupid, but I couldn't stop. I was more and more frightened and began to half-sob, my breath hurting in my chest.

Because I was running with the wind in my ears I didn't hear the river and didn't see it until I burst out on a high bank and nearly ran into space.

I skidded to a stop on the bank, conscious of the river gurgling and grumbling beneath me. There was a fisherman facing me, perhaps 30 feet away, casting to the undercut of the bank I stood on.

As I erupted out of the shrubbery, his eyes widened and there was an instant of alarm before he realized I was just a kid.

Two men flanking me on the riverbank were not as quick to comprehend. With lightning quickness they drew guns and one shouted, "Freeze, goddamit! Don't move! Put your hands behind your head! If you move, I'll kill you!"

I teetered on the bank of the river with the two men pointing large automatic guns at me, their fingers tight on the triggers. I'm going to die! I thought in terror. How can I put my hands behind my head without moving? It was a day of confusion and disruption. Not only had I lost my virginity, but I had lost my way and now I was going to lose my life.

The old man in the river waved at the men and shook his head and said, "Easy, men. Put the guns away." He grinned at me from under a floppy old fisherman's hat. I knew instantly who it was, of course, but it was like seeing the pope at a beer bust or Frank Sinatra dancing with a Birch Lake girl to Art Lundgren and the Jackpine Mellotones.

I was stunned immobile. The old fellow was the President of the United States, Dwight David Eisenhower. "I want to see those hands, Mr. President!" roared one of the men with guns. "Put your hands behind your head!" I slapped my hands against my neck and whinnied with terror.

Ike held up his hand. "Hold on, Pete!" he called to the Secret Service agent who seemed most interested in shooting me. "I don't think we have an assassin here." He waded toward the bank. "You're not involved in some secret assassination plot, are you?" he said.

"N...n...noooo!" I bawled, like a calf in a lightning storm. He stood below me and even in my funk I was uncomfortable looking down at the President. It didn't seem right.

He looked just like his photos, everybody's grandfather, but his eyes were riveting and there was that indefinable something they call "command presence." He grinned again, the grin that got him elected in a landslide, and asked my name and where I was from and I told him, my heart gradually returning to less than 250 beats a second.

"Why are you running around in the woods?" he asked.

One does not lightly lie to the President of the United States, but I didn't want to confess that I was chasing a girl who had seduced me, then had run away. It wasn't what a good soldier would do. So I told him the truth, the whole truth and nothing but the truth, carefully leaving out the middle part where the lies lurked.

"I got lost," I said. "And I guess I got panicky." That was true, believable and enough of the story to satisfy. I told him I thought my canoe was upstream.

"Must be," he said. "You didn't come by here or these cow-boys would have shot it full of holes."

"Sir, I don't know how the hell he got through the security net...." Agent Pete began and Ike interrupted him.

"Well, it looks as if your net has a few holes in it, doesn't it, Pete," Ike said gently, but there was an edge in his voice and Agent Pete flushed.

"Yessir," he said. "It won't happen again. He glared at me, probably wishing he could pump about 500 rounds of hollow-point bullets into little trouble-making me.

"You come here often?" Ike asked.

"Yessir," I said. "I like to trout fish and the Brule is a great river. My rod is back in the canoe."

"Well, I'm not doing so good," he said. "I think I'm spooking them with the line. Never could cast worth a damn."

He gestured, indicating I should climb down to the water's edge. "You think you can show me anything? Let me see you cast."

He handed me Rod One and I gulped. The grip was warm from his hand and I was a foot away from the most powerful man in the world. "Go ahead," he said. It was a Leonard split cane rod, light years ahead of the South Bend hardware store rod I used. It lay in my hand like a fairy wand and I took a moment to admire it. The grip was dark with sweat and use—this president, whether he could cast well or not, cast often.

I stripped some line off, rolled a cast into the current and let the slack pay out. When I had enough line for a full cast I picked it up and dropped his fly, a hopper, into the slick just above the riffle. The fly sank immediately and I stripped it back.

"You cast a good line, son," the president said.

"Could...could I suggest something?" I said hesitantly.

"Hell yes," Ike beamed. "You're my instructor."

"Well, this isn't exactly hopper time, so if it was me, I'd use a little Adams, maybe an 18 and if you have any fly dressing, I'd put some on the wings to keep it from sinking. You have any tippet stuff? This one's pretty heavy."

Ike beamed at Agent Pete, who looked as if he had swallowed a small live frog. "You see, Pete? You guys can shoot, but you can't fish worth a damn." He looked at me. "If you weren't so young I'd hire you to come to Washington and be my fulltime guide."

We sat on a log and he rummaged around in his vest and came up with a spool of two- pound tippet material and I bit off the hopper and tied on a couple of feet of new tippet. Meanwhile, he searched his fly box and found an Adams and handed it to me. "You don't happen to know how to deal with the Russkies too, do you?" he asked.

I shook my head. "Last couple of days I don't think I know how to deal with anyone," I said.

"Bad time?" he asked sympathetically and I nodded. "Tell me about it," he said.

It wasn't an order, but when the President suggests a confession, you'd better start talking. And I wanted to talk about it anyway.

I told him about Jake going crazy and holding up the Quik Fill after some guy from Indiana ran over Jake's cat. And then, like a dam with an ever-increasing breach, I told him about dosing Scuz's pie with maggots and he roared with laughter and nearly fell off the log. "Well, that wasn't bad for you," he said, wiping at his eyes.

"Nossir," I said. "But he got even, kind of." So I told him about Ranger in the parade and how it cost me my girl friend and that brought on another whooping, wheezing fit of laughter. I thought he'd never quit and I hoped to God that I wasn't about to cause the President to have a heart attack from laughing too much. Agent Pete glowered at me, apparently with the same thought.

"I'm sorry for laughing," Ike said, blowing his nose on a big red handkerchief. "But you have to admit it's a pretty funny situation."

"Yeah, I guess so," I said, and then I laughed too, realizing that it really was funny. "Well, anyway, it's been a long weekend and I came up here to kind of get away."

I handed the rod back to Ike and said, "That ought to cast pretty good now. I'd work that eddy line across the river below that big rock."

He waded into the river and stripped line for a cast that collapsed short of the eddy line. "You're dropping your wrist on the backcast sir, er, Mr. President." I said. I raised my arm and showed him what he was doing wrong. "That lets the line fall on the water behind you and you're losing the bend of the rod to shoot the line in front of you. Just keep your wrist stiff so the rod barely goes past straight up. Let the weight of the line bend the rod on the back cast, then just pop it easy and let the line settle down like a little bird."

He lifted the line, but came forward too quickly. "Not so fast," I said. "Let the line straighten out behind you." He tried it again with me talking him through it, and the line floated gently down, a perfect cast. The Adams settled at the very edge of the bubble line and twirled down the current.

A small trout sucked at the fly, but missed and Ike grinned at me and I grinned back. His was the grin that got him elected president. Mine was like the one that lost me my girl friend.

A Secret Service agent came out of the woods and told him he was late for a meeting back at the lodge. "Ah, well, one of the drawbacks of the Presidency," he said. "It cuts into your fishing time."

He turned to Agent Pete and said, "You see that my young fishing instructor here finds his canoe." Agent Pete looked as if he had swallowed another small frog, but nodded assent. Ike unpinned an "I Like Ike" button from his fly vest and handed it to me. "Maybe I'll still be running for president when you're old enough to vote," he said.

He waded across the river and headed up a trail, turned at the bend and waved at me. I waved back. It was the last I saw of him. The button felt like the Congressional Medal of Honor.

"Come on, kid, I haven't got all day," Agent Pete growled.

"Hey, you be careful or I'll tell my fishing buddy on you," I said.

"Shit, kid, don't piss me off or I'll pinch your head off."

We found the canoe about a half-hour later. I made sure I led Agent Pete through a patch of stinging nettle that set him on fire. I smiled at him as the fierce itch made him claw at himself until he drew blood.

I canoed downriver to a state park and hitched a ride back to my truck with an old guy from Iowa who noticed the campaign button and said, "Hey, I heard that Ike is supposed to be fishing the Brule sometime this week. Man, I'd give my left arm to meet him. I been a Republican all my life. Where'd you get that button?"

"Some old guy I met," I said.

"Man, I'd sure like to meet Ike," he said to himself. "I sure do like Ike."

I didn't pull off the highway at Billy Boy Dam, though I glimpsed the ramshackle house through the trees.

It was almost dark when I turned the corner onto Main Street at Jake's Sinclair. There was a sign in the front window: "Closed."

My mother was baking bread and her hands were covered with flour. She hugged me, careful to hold her hands up so they wouldn't get flour on my grimy shirt. "So, how was the trip?" she asked, looking me over. I tried to look like the same old kid.

Great, Mom, I thought. I got laid and taught the President of the United States how to fish. But I didn't say it. "It was a pretty good trip," I said. "But I sure am tired."

She smiled with a hint of sadness in it. "You're still just a boy, no matter what your father thinks," she said. "It was a long trip for a boy."

"A long weekend," I said.

My father came in. "Where'd you get that stupid button?" he growled. He was a lifelong Democrat.

"Some guy up on the Brule was giving them out," I said.

"Hmpfff!" he snorted. "Goddamn Republicans never give up."

I took a long, dreamless nap and when I woke I looked around my room. Everything was there, my Packers and White Sox pennants, the photo of Bob Cousy, the carefully-greased ball glove on the dresser, the airplane mobile, my fly tying vise, my guitar case.

All seemed normal and familiar and everything that had happened might have been a dream except for that "I Like Ike" button.

Quantity discounts are available to your company
or nonprofit for reselling, educational purposes,
subscription incentives, gifts and fundraising campaigns.
For more information, please contact the publisher.

Five Valleys Press
6240 Saint Thomas Dr.
Missoula, Montana 59803
www.FiveValleysPress.com
info@fivevalleyspress.com

About the Author

Joel Vance is a veteran of 21 years as a writer with the Missouri Conservation Department. He has freelanced since the 1960s and has won many writing awards, including the Outdoor Writers Association of America Excellence in Craft Award and also that of the Association of Great Lakes Outdoor Writers. He is a past president of the Outdoor Writers Association of America, has been honored with all three of its major awards (one of only three members so honored in the nearly nine-decade history of the organization, and has been the group's historian).

Vance speaks to a variety of groups on conservation and the environment. He has seven published books. He and his wife Marty live on 40 acres of woods on a dead end road in central Missouri. Wild turkeys are their nearest neighbors.

Vance can be contacted at jvance@socket.net. See also his website www.joelvance.com.